C-2789   CAREER EXAMINATION SERIES

This is your
PASSBOOK for...

Librarian II

Test Preparation Study Guide
Questions & Answers

COPYRIGHT NOTICE

This book is SOLELY intended for, is sold ONLY to, and its use is RESTRICTED to individual, bona fide applicants or candidates who qualify by virtue of having seriously filed applications for appropriate license, certificate, professional and/or promotional advancement, higher school matriculation, scholarship, or other legitimate requirements of education and/or governmental authorities.

This book is NOT intended for use, class instruction, tutoring, training, duplication, copying, reprinting, excerption, or adaptation, etc., by:

1) Other publishers
2) Proprietors and/or Instructors of "Coaching" and/or Preparatory Courses
3) Personnel and/or Training Divisions of commercial, industrial, and governmental organizations
4) Schools, colleges, or universities and/or their departments and staffs, including teachers and other personnel
5) Testing Agencies or Bureaus
6) Study groups which seek by the purchase of a single volume to copy and/or duplicate and/or adapt this material for use by the group as a whole without having purchased individual volumes for each of the members of the group
7) Et al.

Such persons would be in violation of appropriate Federal and State statutes.

PROVISION OF LICENSING AGREEMENTS – Recognized educational, commercial, industrial, and governmental institutions and organizations, and others legitimately engaged in educational pursuits, including training, testing, and measurement activities, may address request for a licensing agreement to the copyright owners, who will determine whether, and under what conditions, including fees and charges, the materials in this book may be used them. In other words, a licensing facility exists for the legitimate use of the material in this book on other than an individual basis. However, it is asseverated and affirmed here that the material in this book CANNOT be used without the receipt of the express permission of such a licensing agreement from the Publishers. Inquiries re licensing should be addressed to the company, attention rights and permissions department.

All rights reserved, including the right of reproduction in whole or in part, in any form or by any means, electronic or mechanical, including photocopying, recording, or by any information storage and retrieval system, without permission in writing from the Publisher.

Copyright © 2024 by
National Learning Corporation

212 Michael Drive, Syosset, NY 11791
(516) 921-8888 • www.passbooks.com
E-mail: info@passbooks.com

PUBLISHED IN THE UNITED STATES OF AMERICA

PASSBOOK® SERIES

THE *PASSBOOK® SERIES* has been created to prepare applicants and candidates for the ultimate academic battlefield – the examination room.

At some time in our lives, each and every one of us may be required to take an examination – for validation, matriculation, admission, qualification, registration, certification, or licensure.

Based on the assumption that every applicant or candidate has met the basic formal educational standards, has taken the required number of courses, and read the necessary texts, the *PASSBOOK® SERIES* furnishes the one special preparation which may assure passing with confidence, instead of failing with insecurity. Examination questions – together with answers – are furnished as the basic vehicle for study so that the mysteries of the examination and its compounding difficulties may be eliminated or diminished by a sure method.

This book is meant to help you pass your examination provided that you qualify and are serious in your objective.

The entire field is reviewed through the huge store of content information which is succinctly presented through a provocative and challenging approach – the question-and-answer method.

A climate of success is established by furnishing the correct answers at the end of each test.

You soon learn to recognize types of questions, forms of questions, and patterns of questioning. You may even begin to anticipate expected outcomes.

You perceive that many questions are repeated or adapted so that you can gain acute insights, which may enable you to score many sure points.

You learn how to confront new questions, or types of questions, and to attack them confidently and work out the correct answers.

You note objectives and emphases, and recognize pitfalls and dangers, so that you may make positive educational adjustments.

Moreover, you are kept fully informed in relation to new concepts, methods, practices, and directions in the field.

You discover that you are actually taking the examination all the time: you are preparing for the examination by "taking" an examination, not by reading extraneous and/or supererogatory textbooks.

In short, this PASSBOOK®, used directedly, should be an important factor in helping you to pass your test.

LIBRARIAN II

DUTIES:
An employee in this class performs professional-level librarian duties in one or more areas of a public library. The work may be specialized in nature or may consist of the more difficult tasks in more than one area. A Librarian II may also serve as a department head in a small library. Supervision may be exercised over professional and nonprofessional staff, and the incumbent may participate in the training of Librarian Trainees. The work is reviewed by a higher-level librarian or administrator through conferences, reports and observation.

EXAMPLES OF TYPICAL TASKS:
Does original cataloging and classification, performs difficult and involved informational and referral services, compiles bibliographies and assists in the selection of library material. Develops and conducts programs for community groups. May supervise subordinate professional or non-professional staff members. Performs related work as required.

SCOPE OF THE EXAMINATION:
The written test will cover knowledge, skills, and/or abilities in such areas as:
1. Library practices and procedures;
2. Supervision;
3. Organizing data into tables and charts; and
4. Information technology and the library.

HOW TO TAKE A TEST

I. YOU MUST PASS AN EXAMINATION

A. *WHAT EVERY CANDIDATE SHOULD KNOW*

Examination applicants often ask us for help in preparing for the written test. What can I study in advance? What kinds of questions will be asked? How will the test be given? How will the papers be graded?

As an applicant for a civil service examination, you may be wondering about some of these things. Our purpose here is to suggest effective methods of advance study and to describe civil service examinations.

Your chances for success on this examination can be increased if you know how to prepare. Those "pre-examination jitters" can be reduced if you know what to expect. You can even experience an adventure in good citizenship if you know why civil service exams are given.

B. *WHY ARE CIVIL SERVICE EXAMINATIONS GIVEN?*

Civil service examinations are important to you in two ways. As a citizen, you want public jobs filled by employees who know how to do their work. As a job seeker, you want a fair chance to compete for that job on an equal footing with other candidates. The best-known means of accomplishing this two-fold goal is the competitive examination.

Exams are widely publicized throughout the nation. They may be administered for jobs in federal, state, city, municipal, town or village governments or agencies.

Any citizen may apply, with some limitations, such as the age or residence of applicants. Your experience and education may be reviewed to see whether you meet the requirements for the particular examination. When these requirements exist, they are reasonable and applied consistently to all applicants. Thus, a competitive examination may cause you some uneasiness now, but it is your privilege and safeguard.

C. *HOW ARE CIVIL SERVICE EXAMS DEVELOPED?*

Examinations are carefully written by trained technicians who are specialists in the field known as "psychological measurement," in consultation with recognized authorities in the field of work that the test will cover. These experts recommend the subject matter areas or skills to be tested; only those knowledges or skills important to your success on the job are included. The most reliable books and source materials available are used as references. Together, the experts and technicians judge the difficulty level of the questions.

Test technicians know how to phrase questions so that the problem is clearly stated. Their ethics do not permit "trick" or "catch" questions. Questions may have been tried out on sample groups, or subjected to statistical analysis, to determine their usefulness.

Written tests are often used in combination with performance tests, ratings of training and experience, and oral interviews. All of these measures combine to form the best-known means of finding the right person for the right job.

II. HOW TO PASS THE WRITTEN TEST

A. NATURE OF THE EXAMINATION

To prepare intelligently for civil service examinations, you should know how they differ from school examinations you have taken. In school you were assigned certain definite pages to read or subjects to cover. The examination questions were quite detailed and usually emphasized memory. Civil service exams, on the other hand, try to discover your present ability to perform the duties of a position, plus your potentiality to learn these duties. In other words, a civil service exam attempts to predict how successful you will be. Questions cover such a broad area that they cannot be as minute and detailed as school exam questions.

In the public service similar kinds of work, or positions, are grouped together in one "class." This process is known as *position-classification*. All the positions in a class are paid according to the salary range for that class. One class title covers all of these positions, and they are all tested by the same examination.

B. FOUR BASIC STEPS

1) Study the announcement

How, then, can you know what subjects to study? Our best answer is: "Learn as much as possible about the class of positions for which you've applied." The exam will test the knowledge, skills and abilities needed to do the work.

Your most valuable source of information about the position you want is the official exam announcement. This announcement lists the training and experience qualifications. Check these standards and apply only if you come reasonably close to meeting them.

The brief description of the position in the examination announcement offers some clues to the subjects which will be tested. Think about the job itself. Review the duties in your mind. Can you perform them, or are there some in which you are rusty? Fill in the blank spots in your preparation.

Many jurisdictions preview the written test in the exam announcement by including a section called "Knowledge and Abilities Required," "Scope of the Examination," or some similar heading. Here you will find out specifically what fields will be tested.

2) Review your own background

Once you learn in general what the position is all about, and what you need to know to do the work, ask yourself which subjects you already know fairly well and which need improvement. You may wonder whether to concentrate on improving your strong areas or on building some background in your fields of weakness. When the announcement has specified "some knowledge" or "considerable knowledge," or has used adjectives like "beginning principles of…" or "advanced … methods," you can get a clue as to the number and difficulty of questions to be asked in any given field. More questions, and hence broader coverage, would be included for those subjects which are more important in the work. Now weigh your strengths and weaknesses against the job requirements and prepare accordingly.

3) Determine the level of the position

Another way to tell how intensively you should prepare is to understand the level of the job for which you are applying. Is it the entering level? In other words, is this the position in which beginners in a field of work are hired? Or is it an intermediate or advanced level? Sometimes this is indicated by such words as "Junior" or "Senior" in the class title. Other jurisdictions use Roman numerals to designate the level – Clerk I, Clerk II, for example. The word "Supervisor" sometimes appears in the title. If the level is not indicated by the title, check the description of duties. Will you be working under very close supervision, or will you have responsibility for independent decisions in this work?

4) Choose appropriate study materials

Now that you know the subjects to be examined and the relative amount of each subject to be covered, you can choose suitable study materials. For beginning level jobs, or even advanced ones, if you have a pronounced weakness in some aspect of your training, read a modern, standard textbook in that field. Be sure it is up to date and has general coverage. Such books are normally available at your library, and the librarian will be glad to help you locate one. For entry-level positions, questions of appropriate difficulty are chosen -- neither highly advanced questions, nor those too simple. Such questions require careful thought but not advanced training.

If the position for which you are applying is technical or advanced, you will read more advanced, specialized material. If you are already familiar with the basic principles of your field, elementary textbooks would waste your time. Concentrate on advanced textbooks and technical periodicals. Think through the concepts and review difficult problems in your field.

These are all general sources. You can get more ideas on your own initiative, following these leads. For example, training manuals and publications of the government agency which employs workers in your field can be useful, particularly for technical and professional positions. A letter or visit to the government department involved may result in more specific study suggestions, and certainly will provide you with a more definite idea of the exact nature of the position you are seeking.

III. KINDS OF TESTS

Tests are used for purposes other than measuring knowledge and ability to perform specified duties. For some positions, it is equally important to test ability to make adjustments to new situations or to profit from training. In others, basic mental abilities not dependent on information are essential. Questions which test these things may not appear as pertinent to the duties of the position as those which test for knowledge and information. Yet they are often highly important parts of a fair examination. For very general questions, it is almost impossible to help you direct your study efforts. What we can do is to point out some of the more common of these general abilities needed in public service positions and describe some typical questions.

1) General information

Broad, general information has been found useful for predicting job success in some kinds of work. This is tested in a variety of ways, from vocabulary lists to questions about current events. Basic background in some field of work, such as sociology or economics, may be sampled in a group of questions. Often these are principles which have become familiar to most persons through exposure rather than through formal training. It is difficult to advise you how to study for these questions; being alert to the world around you is our best suggestion.

2) Verbal ability

An example of an ability needed in many positions is verbal or language ability. Verbal ability is, in brief, the ability to use and understand words. Vocabulary and grammar tests are typical measures of this ability. Reading comprehension or paragraph interpretation questions are common in many kinds of civil service tests. You are given a paragraph of written material and asked to find its central meaning.

3) Numerical ability

Number skills can be tested by the familiar arithmetic problem, by checking paired lists of numbers to see which are alike and which are different, or by interpreting charts and graphs. In the latter test, a graph may be printed in the test booklet which you are asked to use as the basis for answering questions.

4) Observation

A popular test for law-enforcement positions is the observation test. A picture is shown to you for several minutes, then taken away. Questions about the picture test your ability to observe both details and larger elements.

5) Following directions

In many positions in the public service, the employee must be able to carry out written instructions dependably and accurately. You may be given a chart with several columns, each column listing a variety of information. The questions require you to carry out directions involving the information given in the chart.

6) Skills and aptitudes

Performance tests effectively measure some manual skills and aptitudes. When the skill is one in which you are trained, such as typing or shorthand, you can practice. These tests are often very much like those given in business school or high school courses. For many of the other skills and aptitudes, however, no short-time preparation can be made. Skills and abilities natural to you or that you have developed throughout your lifetime are being tested.

Many of the general questions just described provide all the data needed to answer the questions and ask you to use your reasoning ability to find the answers. Your best preparation for these tests, as well as for tests of facts and ideas, is to be at your physical and mental best. You, no doubt, have your own methods of getting into an exam-taking mood and keeping "in shape." The next section lists some ideas on this subject.

IV. KINDS OF QUESTIONS

Only rarely is the "essay" question, which you answer in narrative form, used in civil service tests. Civil service tests are usually of the short-answer type. Full instructions for answering these questions will be given to you at the examination. But in case this is your first experience with short-answer questions and separate answer sheets, here is what you need to know:

1) **Multiple-choice Questions**

Most popular of the short-answer questions is the "multiple choice" or "best answer" question. It can be used, for example, to test for factual knowledge, ability to solve problems or judgment in meeting situations found at work.

A multiple-choice question is normally one of three types—
- It can begin with an incomplete statement followed by several possible endings. You are to find the one ending which *best* completes the statement, although some of the others may not be entirely wrong.
- It can also be a complete statement in the form of a question which is answered by choosing one of the statements listed.

- It can be in the form of a problem – again you select the best answer.

Here is an example of a multiple-choice question with a discussion which should give you some clues as to the method for choosing the right answer:

When an employee has a complaint about his assignment, the action which will *best* help him overcome his difficulty is to
- A. discuss his difficulty with his coworkers
- B. take the problem to the head of the organization
- C. take the problem to the person who gave him the assignment
- D. say nothing to anyone about his complaint

In answering this question, you should study each of the choices to find which is best. Consider choice "A" – Certainly an employee may discuss his complaint with fellow employees, but no change or improvement can result, and the complaint remains unresolved. Choice "B" is a poor choice since the head of the organization probably does not know what assignment you have been given, and taking your problem to him is known as "going over the head" of the supervisor. The supervisor, or person who made the assignment, is the person who can clarify it or correct any injustice. Choice "C" is, therefore, correct. To say nothing, as in choice "D," is unwise. Supervisors have and interest in knowing the problems employees are facing, and the employee is seeking a solution to his problem.

2) True/False Questions

The "true/false" or "right/wrong" form of question is sometimes used. Here a complete statement is given. Your job is to decide whether the statement is right or wrong.

SAMPLE: A roaming cell-phone call to a nearby city costs less than a non-roaming call to a distant city.

This statement is wrong, or false, since roaming calls are more expensive.

This is not a complete list of all possible question forms, although most of the others are variations of these common types. You will always get complete directions for answering questions. Be sure you understand *how* to mark your answers – ask questions until you do.

V. RECORDING YOUR ANSWERS

Computer terminals are used more and more today for many different kinds of exams.

For an examination with very few applicants, you may be told to record your answers in the test booklet itself. Separate answer sheets are much more common. If this separate answer sheet is to be scored by machine – and this is often the case – it is highly important that you mark your answers correctly in order to get credit.

An electronic scoring machine is often used in civil service offices because of the speed with which papers can be scored. Machine-scored answer sheets must be marked with a pencil, which will be given to you. This pencil has a high graphite content which responds to the electronic scoring machine. As a matter of fact, stray dots may register as answers, so do not let your pencil rest on the answer sheet while you are pondering the correct answer. Also, if your pencil lead breaks or is otherwise defective, ask for another.

Since the answer sheet will be dropped in a slot in the scoring machine, be careful not to bend the corners or get the paper crumpled.

The answer sheet normally has five vertical columns of numbers, with 30 numbers to a column. These numbers correspond to the question numbers in your test booklet. After each number, going across the page are four or five pairs of dotted lines. These short dotted lines have small letters or numbers above them. The first two pairs may also have a "T" or "F" above the letters. This indicates that the first two pairs only are to be used if the questions are of the true-false type. If the questions are multiple choice, disregard the "T" and "F" and pay attention only to the small letters or numbers.

Answer your questions in the manner of the sample that follows:

32. The largest city in the United States is
    A. Washington, D.C.
    B. New York City
    C. Chicago
    D. Detroit
    E. San Francisco

1) Choose the answer you think is best. (New York City is the largest, so "B" is correct.)
2) Find the row of dotted lines numbered the same as the question you are answering. (Find row number 32)
3) Find the pair of dotted lines corresponding to the answer. (Find the pair of lines under the mark "B.")
4) Make a solid black mark between the dotted lines.

VI. BEFORE THE TEST

Common sense will help you find procedures to follow to get ready for an examination. Too many of us, however, overlook these sensible measures. Indeed, nervousness and fatigue have been found to be the most serious reasons why applicants fail to do their best on civil service tests. Here is a list of reminders:

- Begin your preparation early – Don't wait until the last minute to go scurrying around for books and materials or to find out what the position is all about.
- Prepare continuously – An hour a night for a week is better than an all-night cram session. This has been definitely established. What is more, a night a week for a month will return better dividends than crowding your study into a shorter period of time.
- Locate the place of the exam – You have been sent a notice telling you when and where to report for the examination. If the location is in a different town or otherwise unfamiliar to you, it would be well to inquire the best route and learn something about the building.
- Relax the night before the test – Allow your mind to rest. Do not study at all that night. Plan some mild recreation or diversion; then go to bed early and get a good night's sleep.
- Get up early enough to make a leisurely trip to the place for the test – This way unforeseen events, traffic snarls, unfamiliar buildings, etc. will not upset you.
- Dress comfortably – A written test is not a fashion show. You will be known by number and not by name, so wear something comfortable.

- Leave excess paraphernalia at home – Shopping bags and odd bundles will get in your way. You need bring only the items mentioned in the official notice you received; usually everything you need is provided. Do not bring reference books to the exam. They will only confuse those last minutes and be taken away from you when in the test room.
- Arrive somewhat ahead of time – If because of transportation schedules you must get there very early, bring a newspaper or magazine to take your mind off yourself while waiting.
- Locate the examination room – When you have found the proper room, you will be directed to the seat or part of the room where you will sit. Sometimes you are given a sheet of instructions to read while you are waiting. Do not fill out any forms until you are told to do so; just read them and be prepared.
- Relax and prepare to listen to the instructions
- If you have any physical problem that may keep you from doing your best, be sure to tell the test administrator. If you are sick or in poor health, you really cannot do your best on the exam. You can come back and take the test some other time.

VII. AT THE TEST

The day of the test is here and you have the test booklet in your hand. The temptation to get going is very strong. Caution! There is more to success than knowing the right answers. You must know how to identify your papers and understand variations in the type of short-answer question used in this particular examination. Follow these suggestions for maximum results from your efforts:

1) Cooperate with the monitor

The test administrator has a duty to create a situation in which you can be as much at ease as possible. He will give instructions, tell you when to begin, check to see that you are marking your answer sheet correctly, and so on. He is not there to guard you, although he will see that your competitors do not take unfair advantage. He wants to help you do your best.

2) Listen to all instructions

Don't jump the gun! Wait until you understand all directions. In most civil service tests you get more time than you need to answer the questions. So don't be in a hurry. Read each word of instructions until you clearly understand the meaning. Study the examples, listen to all announcements and follow directions. Ask questions if you do not understand what to do.

3) Identify your papers

Civil service exams are usually identified by number only. You will be assigned a number; you must not put your name on your test papers. Be sure to copy your number correctly. Since more than one exam may be given, copy your exact examination title.

4) Plan your time

Unless you are told that a test is a "speed" or "rate of work" test, speed itself is usually not important. Time enough to answer all the questions will be provided, but this does not mean that you have all day. An overall time limit has been set. Divide the total time (in minutes) by the number of questions to determine the approximate time you have for each question.

5) Do not linger over difficult questions

If you come across a difficult question, mark it with a paper clip (useful to have along) and come back to it when you have been through the booklet. One caution if you do this – be sure to skip a number on your answer sheet as well. Check often to be sure that you have not lost your place and that you are marking in the row numbered the same as the question you are answering.

6) Read the questions

Be sure you know what the question asks! Many capable people are unsuccessful because they failed to *read* the questions correctly.

7) Answer all questions

Unless you have been instructed that a penalty will be deducted for incorrect answers, it is better to guess than to omit a question.

8) Speed tests

It is often better NOT to guess on speed tests. It has been found that on timed tests people are tempted to spend the last few seconds before time is called in marking answers at random – without even reading them – in the hope of picking up a few extra points. To discourage this practice, the instructions may warn you that your score will be "corrected" for guessing. That is, a penalty will be applied. The incorrect answers will be deducted from the correct ones, or some other penalty formula will be used.

9) Review your answers

If you finish before time is called, go back to the questions you guessed or omitted to give them further thought. Review other answers if you have time.

10) Return your test materials

If you are ready to leave before others have finished or time is called, take ALL your materials to the monitor and leave quietly. Never take any test material with you. The monitor can discover whose papers are not complete, and taking a test booklet may be grounds for disqualification.

VIII. EXAMINATION TECHNIQUES

1) Read the general instructions carefully. These are usually printed on the first page of the exam booklet. As a rule, these instructions refer to the timing of the examination; the fact that you should not start work until the signal and must stop work at a signal, etc. If there are any *special* instructions, such as a choice of questions to be answered, make sure that you note this instruction carefully.

2) When you are ready to start work on the examination, that is as soon as the signal has been given, read the instructions to each question booklet, underline any key words or phrases, such as *least, best, outline, describe* and the like. In this way you will tend to answer as requested rather than discover on reviewing your paper that you *listed without describing*, that you selected the *worst* choice rather than the *best* choice, etc.

3) If the examination is of the objective or multiple-choice type – that is, each question will also give a series of possible answers: A, B, C or D, and you are called upon to select the best answer and write the letter next to that answer on your answer paper – it is advisable to start answering each question in turn. There may be anywhere from 50 to 100 such questions in the three or four hours allotted and you can see how much time would be taken if you read through all the questions before beginning to answer any. Furthermore, if you come across a question or group of questions which you know would be difficult to answer, it would undoubtedly affect your handling of all the other questions.

4) If the examination is of the essay type and contains but a few questions, it is a moot point as to whether you should read all the questions before starting to answer any one. Of course, if you are given a choice – say five out of seven and the like – then it is essential to read all the questions so you can eliminate the two that are most difficult. If, however, you are asked to answer all the questions, there may be danger in trying to answer the easiest one first because you may find that you will spend too much time on it. The best technique is to answer the first question, then proceed to the second, etc.

5) Time your answers. Before the exam begins, write down the time it started, then add the time allowed for the examination and write down the time it must be completed, then divide the time available somewhat as follows:
    - If 3-1/2 hours are allowed, that would be 210 minutes. If you have 80 objective-type questions, that would be an average of 2-1/2 minutes per question. Allow yourself no more than 2 minutes per question, or a total of 160 minutes, which will permit about 50 minutes to review.
    - If for the time allotment of 210 minutes there are 7 essay questions to answer, that would average about 30 minutes a question. Give yourself only 25 minutes per question so that you have about 35 minutes to review.

6) The most important instruction is to *read each question* and make sure you know what is wanted. The second most important instruction is to *time yourself properly* so that you answer every question. The third most important instruction is to *answer every question*. Guess if you have to but include something for each question. Remember that you will receive no credit for a blank and will probably receive some credit if you write something in answer to an essay question. If you guess a letter – say "B" for a multiple-choice question – you may have guessed right. If you leave a blank as an answer to a multiple-choice question, the examiners may respect your feelings but it will not add a point to your score. Some exams may penalize you for wrong answers, so in such cases *only*, you may not want to guess unless you have some basis for your answer.

7) Suggestions
    a. Objective-type questions
        1. Examine the question booklet for proper sequence of pages and questions
        2. Read all instructions carefully
        3. Skip any question which seems too difficult; return to it after all other questions have been answered
        4. Apportion your time properly; do not spend too much time on any single question or group of questions

5. Note and underline key words – *all, most, fewest, least, best, worst, same, opposite*, etc.
6. Pay particular attention to negatives
7. Note unusual option, e.g., unduly long, short, complex, different or similar in content to the body of the question
8. Observe the use of "hedging" words – *probably, may, most likely,* etc.
9. Make sure that your answer is put next to the same number as the question
10. Do not second-guess unless you have good reason to believe the second answer is definitely more correct
11. Cross out original answer if you decide another answer is more accurate; do not erase until you are ready to hand your paper in
12. Answer all questions; guess unless instructed otherwise
13. Leave time for review

   b. Essay questions
1. Read each question carefully
2. Determine exactly what is wanted. Underline key words or phrases.
3. Decide on outline or paragraph answer
4. Include many different points and elements unless asked to develop any one or two points or elements
5. Show impartiality by giving pros and cons unless directed to select one side only
6. Make and write down any assumptions you find necessary to answer the questions
7. Watch your English, grammar, punctuation and choice of words
8. Time your answers; don't crowd material

8) Answering the essay question

Most essay questions can be answered by framing the specific response around several key words or ideas. Here are a few such key words or ideas:

M's: manpower, materials, methods, money, management
P's: purpose, program, policy, plan, procedure, practice, problems, pitfalls, personnel, public relations
   a. Six basic steps in handling problems:
1. Preliminary plan and background development
2. Collect information, data and facts
3. Analyze and interpret information, data and facts
4. Analyze and develop solutions as well as make recommendations
5. Prepare report and sell recommendations
6. Install recommendations and follow up effectiveness

   b. Pitfalls to avoid
1. *Taking things for granted* – A statement of the situation does not necessarily imply that each of the elements is necessarily true; for example, a complaint may be invalid and biased so that all that can be taken for granted is that a complaint has been registered

2. *Considering only one side of a situation* – Wherever possible, indicate several alternatives and then point out the reasons you selected the best one
3. *Failing to indicate follow up* – Whenever your answer indicates action on your part, make certain that you will take proper follow-up action to see how successful your recommendations, procedures or actions turn out to be
4. *Taking too long in answering any single question* – Remember to time your answers properly

IX. AFTER THE TEST

Scoring procedures differ in detail among civil service jurisdictions although the general principles are the same. Whether the papers are hand-scored or graded by machine we have described, they are nearly always graded by number. That is, the person who marks the paper knows only the number – never the name – of the applicant. Not until all the papers have been graded will they be matched with names. If other tests, such as training and experience or oral interview ratings have been given, scores will be combined. Different parts of the examination usually have different weights. For example, the written test might count 60 percent of the final grade, and a rating of training and experience 40 percent. In many jurisdictions, veterans will have a certain number of points added to their grades.

After the final grade has been determined, the names are placed in grade order and an eligible list is established. There are various methods for resolving ties between those who get the same final grade – probably the most common is to place first the name of the person whose application was received first. Job offers are made from the eligible list in the order the names appear on it. You will be notified of your grade and your rank as soon as all these computations have been made. This will be done as rapidly as possible.

People who are found to meet the requirements in the announcement are called "eligibles." Their names are put on a list of eligible candidates. An eligible's chances of getting a job depend on how high he stands on this list and how fast agencies are filling jobs from the list.

When a job is to be filled from a list of eligibles, the agency asks for the names of people on the list of eligibles for that job. When the civil service commission receives this request, it sends to the agency the names of the three people highest on this list. Or, if the job to be filled has specialized requirements, the office sends the agency the names of the top three persons who meet these requirements from the general list.

The appointing officer makes a choice from among the three people whose names were sent to him. If the selected person accepts the appointment, the names of the others are put back on the list to be considered for future openings.

That is the rule in hiring from all kinds of eligible lists, whether they are for typist, carpenter, chemist, or something else. For every vacancy, the appointing officer has his choice of any one of the top three eligibles on the list. This explains why the person whose name is on top of the list sometimes does not get an appointment when some of the persons lower on the list do. If the appointing officer chooses the second or third eligible, the No. 1 eligible does not get a job at once, but stays on the list until he is appointed or the list is terminated.

X. HOW TO PASS THE INTERVIEW TEST

The examination for which you applied requires an oral interview test. You have already taken the written test and you are now being called for the interview test – the final part of the formal examination.

You may think that it is not possible to prepare for an interview test and that there are no procedures to follow during an interview. Our purpose is to point out some things you can do in advance that will help you and some good rules to follow and pitfalls to avoid while you are being interviewed.

What is an interview supposed to test?

The written examination is designed to test the technical knowledge and competence of the candidate; the oral is designed to evaluate intangible qualities, not readily measured otherwise, and to establish a list showing the relative fitness of each candidate – as measured against his competitors – for the position sought. Scoring is not on the basis of "right" and "wrong," but on a sliding scale of values ranging from "not passable" to "outstanding." As a matter of fact, it is possible to achieve a relatively low score without a single "incorrect" answer because of evident weakness in the qualities being measured.

Occasionally, an examination may consist entirely of an oral test – either an individual or a group oral. In such cases, information is sought concerning the technical knowledges and abilities of the candidate, since there has been no written examination for this purpose. More commonly, however, an oral test is used to supplement a written examination.

Who conducts interviews?

The composition of oral boards varies among different jurisdictions. In nearly all, a representative of the personnel department serves as chairman. One of the members of the board may be a representative of the department in which the candidate would work. In some cases, "outside experts" are used, and, frequently, a businessman or some other representative of the general public is asked to serve. Labor and management or other special groups may be represented. The aim is to secure the services of experts in the appropriate field.

However the board is composed, it is a good idea (and not at all improper or unethical) to ascertain in advance of the interview who the members are and what groups they represent. When you are introduced to them, you will have some idea of their backgrounds and interests, and at least you will not stutter and stammer over their names.

What should be done before the interview?

While knowledge about the board members is useful and takes some of the surprise element out of the interview, there is other preparation which is more substantive. It *is* possible to prepare for an oral interview – in several ways:

1) Keep a copy of your application and review it carefully before the interview

This may be the only document before the oral board, and the starting point of the interview. Know what education and experience you have listed there, and the sequence and dates of all of it. Sometimes the board will ask you to review the highlights of your experience for them; you should not have to hem and haw doing it.

2) Study the class specification and the examination announcement

Usually, the oral board has one or both of these to guide them. The qualities, characteristics or knowledges required by the position sought are stated in these documents. They offer valuable clues as to the nature of the oral interview. For example, if the job involves supervisory responsibilities, the announcement will usually indicate that knowledge of modern supervisory methods and the qualifications of the candidate as a supervisor will be tested. If so, you can expect such questions, frequently in the form of a hypothetical situation which you are expected to solve. NEVER go into an oral without knowledge of the duties and responsibilities of the job you seek.

3) Think through each qualification required
Try to visualize the kind of questions you would ask if you were a board member. How well could you answer them? Try especially to appraise your own knowledge and background in each area, *measured against the job sought*, and identify any areas in which you are weak. Be critical and realistic – do not flatter yourself.

4) Do some general reading in areas in which you feel you may be weak
For example, if the job involves supervision and your past experience has NOT, some general reading in supervisory methods and practices, particularly in the field of human relations, might be useful. Do NOT study agency procedures or detailed manuals. The oral board will be testing your understanding and capacity, not your memory.

5) Get a good night's sleep and watch your general health and mental attitude
You will want a clear head at the interview. Take care of a cold or any other minor ailment, and of course, no hangovers.

What should be done on the day of the interview?
Now comes the day of the interview itself. Give yourself plenty of time to get there. Plan to arrive somewhat ahead of the scheduled time, particularly if your appointment is in the fore part of the day. If a previous candidate fails to appear, the board might be ready for you a bit early. By early afternoon an oral board is almost invariably behind schedule if there are many candidates, and you may have to wait. Take along a book or magazine to read, or your application to review, but leave any extraneous material in the waiting room when you go in for your interview. In any event, relax and compose yourself.

The matter of dress is important. The board is forming impressions about you – from your experience, your manners, your attitude, and your appearance. Give your personal appearance careful attention. Dress your best, but not your flashiest. Choose conservative, appropriate clothing, and be sure it is immaculate. This is a business interview, and your appearance should indicate that you regard it as such. Besides, being well groomed and properly dressed will help boost your confidence.

Sooner or later, someone will call your name and escort you into the interview room. *This is it.* From here on you are on your own. It is too late for any more preparation. But remember, you asked for this opportunity to prove your fitness, and you are here because your request was granted.

What happens when you go in?
The usual sequence of events will be as follows: The clerk (who is often the board stenographer) will introduce you to the chairman of the oral board, who will introduce you to the other members of the board. Acknowledge the introductions before you sit down. Do not be surprised if you find a microphone facing you or a stenotypist sitting by. Oral interviews are usually recorded in the event of an appeal or other review.

Usually the chairman of the board will open the interview by reviewing the highlights of your education and work experience from your application – primarily for the benefit of the other members of the board, as well as to get the material into the record. Do not interrupt or comment unless there is an error or significant misinterpretation; if that is the case, do not hesitate. But do not quibble about insignificant matters. Also, he will usually ask you some question about your education, experience or your present job – partly to get you to start talking and to establish the interviewing "rapport." He may start the actual questioning, or turn it over to one of the other members. Frequently, each member undertakes the questioning on a particular area, one in which he is perhaps most competent, so you can expect each member to participate in the examination. Because time is limited, you may also expect some rather abrupt switches in the direction the questioning takes, so do not be upset by it. Normally, a board member will not pursue a single line of questioning unless he discovers a particular strength or weakness.

After each member has participated, the chairman will usually ask whether any member has any further questions, then will ask you if you have anything you wish to add. Unless you are expecting this question, it may floor you. Worse, it may start you off on an extended, extemporaneous speech. The board is not usually seeking more information. The question is principally to offer you a last opportunity to present further qualifications or to indicate that you have nothing to add. So, if you feel that a significant qualification or characteristic has been overlooked, it is proper to point it out in a sentence or so. Do not compliment the board on the thoroughness of their examination -- they have been sketchy, and you know it. If you wish, merely say, "No thank you, I have nothing further to add." This is a point where you can "talk yourself out" of a good impression or fail to present an important bit of information. Remember, *you close the interview yourself*.

The chairman will then say, "That is all, Mr. _____, thank you." Do not be startled; the interview is over, and quicker than you think. Thank him, gather your belongings and take your leave. Save your sigh of relief for the other side of the door.

How to put your best foot forward
Throughout this entire process, you may feel that the board individually and collectively is trying to pierce your defenses, seek out your hidden weaknesses and embarrass and confuse you. Actually, this is not true. They are obliged to make an appraisal of your qualifications for the job you are seeking, and they want to see you in your best light. Remember, they must interview all candidates and a non-cooperative candidate may become a failure in spite of their best efforts to bring out his qualifications. Here are 15 suggestions that will help you:

1) **Be natural – Keep your attitude confident, not cocky**
If you are not confident that you can do the job, do not expect the board to be. Do not apologize for your weaknesses, try to bring out your strong points. The board is interested in a positive, not negative, presentation. Cockiness will antagonize any board member and make him wonder if you are covering up a weakness by a false show of strength.

2) **Get comfortable, but don't lounge or sprawl**
Sit erectly but not stiffly. A careless posture may lead the board to conclude that you are careless in other things, or at least that you are not impressed by the importance of the occasion. Either conclusion is natural, even if incorrect. Do not fuss with your clothing, a pencil or an ashtray. Your hands may occasionally be useful to emphasize a point; do not let them become a point of distraction.

3) **Do not wisecrack or make small talk**
This is a serious situation, and your attitude should show that you consider it as such. Further, the time of the board is limited – they do not want to waste it, and neither should you.

4) Do not exaggerate your experience or abilities

In the first place, from information in the application or other interviews and sources, the board may know more about you than you think. Secondly, you probably will not get away with it. An experienced board is rather adept at spotting such a situation, so do not take the chance.

5) If you know a board member, do not make a point of it, yet do not hide it

Certainly you are not fooling him, and probably not the other members of the board. Do not try to take advantage of your acquaintanceship – it will probably do you little good.

6) Do not dominate the interview

Let the board do that. They will give you the clues – do not assume that you have to do all the talking. Realize that the board has a number of questions to ask you, and do not try to take up all the interview time by showing off your extensive knowledge of the answer to the first one.

7) Be attentive

You only have 20 minutes or so, and you should keep your attention at its sharpest throughout. When a member is addressing a problem or question to you, give him your undivided attention. Address your reply principally to him, but do not exclude the other board members.

8) Do not interrupt

A board member may be stating a problem for you to analyze. He will ask you a question when the time comes. Let him state the problem, and wait for the question.

9) Make sure you understand the question

Do not try to answer until you are sure what the question is. If it is not clear, restate it in your own words or ask the board member to clarify it for you. However, do not haggle about minor elements.

10) Reply promptly but not hastily

A common entry on oral board rating sheets is "candidate responded readily," or "candidate hesitated in replies." Respond as promptly and quickly as you can, but do not jump to a hasty, ill-considered answer.

11) Do not be peremptory in your answers

A brief answer is proper – but do not fire your answer back. That is a losing game from your point of view. The board member can probably ask questions much faster than you can answer them.

12) Do not try to create the answer you think the board member wants

He is interested in what kind of mind you have and how it works – not in playing games. Furthermore, he can usually spot this practice and will actually grade you down on it.

13) Do not switch sides in your reply merely to agree with a board member

Frequently, a member will take a contrary position merely to draw you out and to see if you are willing and able to defend your point of view. Do not start a debate, yet do not surrender a good position. If a position is worth taking, it is worth defending.

14) Do not be afraid to admit an error in judgment if you are shown to be wrong

The board knows that you are forced to reply without any opportunity for careful consideration. Your answer may be demonstrably wrong. If so, admit it and get on with the interview.

15) Do not dwell at length on your present job

The opening question may relate to your present assignment. Answer the question but do not go into an extended discussion. You are being examined for a *new* job, not your present one. As a matter of fact, try to phrase ALL your answers in terms of the job for which you are being examined.

Basis of Rating

Probably you will forget most of these "do's" and "don'ts" when you walk into the oral interview room. Even remembering them all will not ensure you a passing grade. Perhaps you did not have the qualifications in the first place. But remembering them will help you to put your best foot forward, without treading on the toes of the board members.

Rumor and popular opinion to the contrary notwithstanding, an oral board wants you to make the best appearance possible. They know you are under pressure – but they also want to see how you respond to it as a guide to what your reaction would be under the pressures of the job you seek. They will be influenced by the degree of poise you display, the personal traits you show and the manner in which you respond.

ABOUT THIS BOOK

This book contains tests divided into Examination Sections. Go through each test, answering every question in the margin. We have also attached a sample answer sheet at the back of the book that can be removed and used. At the end of each test look at the answer key and check your answers. On the ones you got wrong, look at the right answer choice and learn. Do not fill in the answers first. Do not memorize the questions and answers, but understand the answer and principles involved. On your test, the questions will likely be different from the samples. Questions are changed and new ones added. If you understand these past questions you should have success with any changes that arise. Tests may consist of several types of questions. We have additional books on each subject should more study be advisable or necessary for you. Finally, the more you study, the better prepared you will be. This book is intended to be the last thing you study before you walk into the examination room. Prior study of relevant texts is also recommended. NLC publishes some of these in our Fundamental Series. Knowledge and good sense are important factors in passing your exam. Good luck also helps. So now study this Passbook, absorb the material contained within and take that knowledge into the examination. Then do your best to pass that exam.

EXAMINATION SECTION

EXAMINATION SECTION
TEST 1

DIRECTIONS: Each question or incomplete statement is followed by several suggested answers or completions. Select the one the BEST answers the question or completes the statement. *PRINT THE LETTER OF THE CORRECT ANSWER IN THE SPACE AT THE RIGHT.*

1. The publication *Information Power: Building Partnerships for Learning* focuses standards for library media programs on the   1.____

    A. equipment, as well as the media
    B. learner
    C. collection
    D. school

2. The Internet has changed reference services in a number of ways, both positive and negative. Negative effects include each of the following, EXCEPT   2.____

    A. increased likelihood of encountering false or misleading information
    B. the possibility of confusing information seekers through the sheer numbers of results found in Internet searches
    C. greater time demands on library media specialists in responding to student requests for information
    D. the possibility of over-reliance on electronic resources when print reference materials offer faster access

3. Which of the following would be defined as "capital outlays" in a library media center's budget?   3.____

    A. Audiovisual materials
    B. Office supplies
    C. Copy machines
    D. Books

4. The foremost concern in the planning, selection, and purchase of library media center collections should be   4.____

    A. breadth
    B. quantity
    C. cost
    D. balance

5. Which of the following Internet search tools is considered a directory, rather than a search engine?   5.____

    A. Lycos
    B. Northern Light
    C. Yahoo
    D. Google

6. A high school computer science teacher has asked the library media specialist to locate materials for a unit on artificial intelligence. After a thorough search, the media specialist finds that the only available materials are too costly or too complex for secondary students. The library media specialist should

    A. help the instructor locate and apply for grant funding
    B. recommend another, less obscure area of study
    C. write to a large software manufacturer requesting a donation for the purchase of materials
    D. offer to help the instructor develop original instructional materials

7. A comprehensive evaluation of the media center's program demonstrates that the size of the book collection is inadequate when compared to the high-service examples set forth in the ALA's *Information Power*. The media specialist's first step would be to present the evaluation's findings to the

    A. district media supervisor
    B. school principal
    C. parent-teacher association
    D. library media advisory committee

8. As a general rule, the reading and browsing area of a library media center should be provided with seating for a minimum of _____ % of the student body.

    A. 15
    B. 30
    C. 45
    D. 60

9. A Dewey number that begins with 567 would mark an item that deals with the subject of

    A. fine arts
    B. science
    C. history
    D. social sciences

10. Together, a high school social studies teacher and a library media specialist are writing instructional objectives for a unit on media bias. Which of the following verbs identifies a skill that is in the "analyzing" category of learning tasks?

    A. Define
    B. Classify
    C. Discriminate
    D. Create

11. A multimedia kit is LEAST likely to include

    A. small models of objects
    B. a small computer
    C. audiocassettes
    D. a duplicable folder of activity sheets

12. In library media centers, the Americans with Disabilities Act (ADA) recommends a space of _____ inches between shelving units, and mandates a minimum space of _____ inches.

    A. 36; 24
    B. 42; 36
    C. 50; 42
    D. 72; 50

13. Which of the following is NOT a guideline that should be followed in the design of a new library media center?

    A. The media center should have its own outside entrance, or be located near one, so that it is accessible before, during, and after school without security problems
    B. Restroom facilities should be available within the secured area
    C. Unimpeded physical access to all areas of the library media center should be provided for special needs users
    D. Office space should be open and integrated with student work areas in order to ensure supervision and conviviality

14. Freedom of speech is an ethical issue in the digital age because

    A. the use of some Internet technology violates the privacy of others
    B. only people who have some technical proficiency can express their views on-line
    C. it is impossible to enforce what people can and cannot say on the Internet
    D. the censorship of views expressed on the Internet may be a violation of civil rights

15. Authoring systems

    A. are rarely used in schools because of sophisticated hardware requirements
    B. enable an instructor to create customized computer-enhanced lessons
    C. require an instructor to know at least one simple computer programming language
    D. require high-speed Internet access

16. A library media center wants to participate in a statewide shared database of library media center materials. Most likely, this will involve a commitment to

    A. developing written protocols for using the network
    B. purchasing multiple terminals
    C. training staff in the use of electronic catalogs
    D. using a standard bibliographic record

17. A student is working on an essay for his social studies class. He has used the word "justice," in a sentence, but thinks the word might not be appropriate for the context in which it appears. The library media specialist should refer the student to

    A. *Roget's Thesaurus*
    B. *Black's Law Dictionary*
    C. the *World Book Encyclopedia*
    D. the *American Heritage Dictionary*

18. Which of the following is a nonfiction author?

    A. Naomi Shahib Nye
    B. Linda Sue Park
    C. Gail Gibbons
    D. Graham Salisbury

19. Which of the following criteria would probably be LEAST helpful in the process of collection evaluation?

    A. Integration of information formats
    B. Student and teacher needs
    C. Alignment with curriculum
    D. Concordance with other collections in similar facilities

20. A library media specialist has been hired to take over the media center at a large suburban middle school. The media center has been operated for several years on the fixed-schedule system, and the principal has insisted on retaining this system for the time being. As a first step, the library media specialist should

    A. set up the scheduled classes but allow free time every day when students can come to the media center from any class for any information need
    B. appeal to the library media coordinator at the district level, if there is one, to help guide the principal to a change in policy
    C. prepare an outline of the growing research and professional opinion indicating the advantages of flexible scheduling
    D. circulate an appeal among classroom teachers to advocate for a change to flexible scheduling

21. Cards in a library catalog are filed according to rules established by the

    A. American Library Association (ALA)
    B. Association for Educational Communications and Technology (AECT)
    C. Library of Congress
    D. American Association of School Librarians (AASL)

22. Which of the following companies offers an on-line subscription service for librarians?

    A. Information Plus
    B. Haworth Press
    C. H. W. Wilson
    D. Brodart

23. Usually, a library media center's weeding process begins with the identification of

    A. physical condition of items
    B. copyright dates
    C. teachers' stated preferences for removal
    D. circulation records

24. A library media specialist at an elementary school is working to tailor the media center's program to fit the school's. Which of the following questions is appropriate for the specialist to consider as she goes through this process?

    I. How are students grouped?
    II. How are activities scheduled?
    III. What instructional methods are preferred by teachers?
    IV. What are the major concepts of elementary school education?

    A. I and II
    B. I, II, and IV
    C. III only
    D. I, II, III and IV

25. Educational programs for school library media specialists are accredited by the
    I. National Association of State Directors of Teacher Education Certification (NASDTEC)
    II. National Council for the Accreditation of Teacher Education (NCATE)
    III. National Board for Professional Teaching Standards (NBPTS)
    IV. American Association of School Librarians (AASL)

    A. I only
    B. I and II
    C. II and III
    D. I, II, III and IV

KEY (CORRECT ANSWERS)

1.	B		11.	B
2.	C		12.	B
3.	C		13.	D
4.	D		14.	D
5.	C		15.	B
6.	D		16.	D
7.	B		17.	A
8.	A		18.	C
9.	B		19.	D
10.	C		20.	A

21. A
22. C
23. D
24. D
25. B

TEST 2

DIRECTIONS: Each question or incomplete statement is followed by several suggested answers or completions. Select the one the BEST answers the question or completes the statement. *PRINT THE LETTER OF THE CORRECT ANSWER IN THE SPACE AT THE RIGHT.*

1. A library media specialist at a small rural public library does not have an automated system, and must create catalog cards on the computer. Guidelines for creating one's own cards include each of the following, EXCEPT

    A. When there is more than one author, place only the first one on the top line.
    B. Capitalize only the first word in the title and those that are proper names.
    C. If there is no author, begin with the publisher.
    D. Type subject headings in all capital letters.

2. A student is looking for the full text of articles about the historical significance of the writer James Baldwin and his work. The best resource for this inquiry would be

    A. *Oxford Companion to African American Literature*
    B. *MLA International Bibliography*
    C. *Scribner Writers Series*
    D. *Encyclopedia Britannica*

3. A library media specialist is planning a seminar for teachers on the use of a new projection device for PCs. The most effective way to present the seminar would be to

    A. conduct small-groups demonstrations with hands-on practice
    B. show a videotape about how to use the device
    C. hire an expert to demonstrate the device at a faculty meeting
    D. develop diagrams of the device for distribution at the workshop

4. In the past two decades, user behaviors at school library media centers have generally changed in each of the following ways, EXCEPT becoming more

    A. format-oriented than information-oriented
    B. focused on widely available on-line access
    C. curriculum-integrated
    D. focused on information access than library skills

5. Which of the following would be the most appropriate software application for creating and managing student records?

    A. Spreadsheet
    B. Word processing
    C. Database
    D. Presentation

6. A library media center's collection development policy should include each of the following, EXCEPT

    A. acquisition policies
    B. selection criteria
    C. school objectives
    D. current equipment costs

7. In presenting budget proposals to school and district administrators, a library media center's justification for spending should be stated in terms of

   A. a comparative analysis of spending on other schools in the region of similar size and student needs
   B. a comparison between the services the library media center is mandated to perform, given its mission statement, and what it has been able to perform given its resource levels
   C. expressions of support for the library media center from students, parents, and faculty
   D. how well learning goals and objectives for the total school's instructional program are realized through the library media center

8. At the district level, the policies that have the greatest impact on a school's library media program are those concerning the

   A. purchasing of textbooks
   B. maintenance of student records
   C. selection of materials
   D. provision of in-service education

9. In areas of the library media center where visual supervision is needed, book shelving at a height of _____ inches is generally recommended.

   A. 24
   B. 42
   C. 60
   D. 72

10. Internet resources should be evaluated in much the same way as print resources. However, the criteria for Internet resources often require different levels of scrutiny on the part of the library media specialist. In particular, the criterion of _____ is one that should be given more attention when evaluating Internet resources.

    A. purpose
    B. audience
    C. scope
    D. authority

11. In selecting materials for young people, the best resource would be

    A. *Junior High School Catalog*
    B. *How to Find Out About Children's Literature*
    C. *Folklore for Children and Young People*
    D. *Best Science Books for Children*

12. Which of the following is a significant difference between a GIF file and a JPEG file?

    A. JPEGs are used for color images; GIFs for grayscale
    B. JPEGs offer better image resolution
    C. GIF is a North American file format
    D. GIFs are specific to Macintosh software; JPEGs to Windows

13. The organization that develops national standards for the evaluation of school library media center collections is the

    A. American Library Association (ALA)
    B. U.S. Department of Education
    C. National Coalition for Literacy
    D. American Association of School Librarians (AASL)

14. A library media specialist wants to acquire a single on-line portal for on-line reference resources, bibliographic databases, and subscriptions.
    Which of the following vendors is MOST appropriate for this application?

    A. Gale Research
    B. EBSCO Information Services
    C. Follet Library Resources
    D. Greenwood Publishing

15. Guidelines for creating an aesthetically pleasing environment in the library media center include
    I. harmonious color schemes
    II. signage, including Braille, to clearly indicate the location of information
    III. provision for unobtrusive security during service hours
    IV. combined activity and study areas

    A. I only
    B. I, II and III
    C. II and III
    D. I, II, III and IV

16. Which of the following is NOT a general Internet directory resource?

    A. World Biographical Index
    B. CyberDewey
    C. Yahoo
    D. About.com

17. In the case of a copyright infringement, the _____ can be sued by the owner of a copyright.
    I. media specialist
    II. teacher
    III. principal
    IV. school board

    A. I only
    B. I and II
    C. I, II and III
    D. I, II, III and IV

18. In the school library media center budgeting process, most purchase orders are expected to be obligated by no later than

    A. April 1
    B. June 30
    C. October 31
    D. January 1

19. Which of the following Top Level Domains (TDLs) in an Internet address used by non-profit organizations?

    A. .np
    B. .org
    C. .net
    D. .int

20. Roles of volunteer personnel in a large library media center are LEAST likely to include

    A. circulating materials
    B. shelving resources
    C. loading records into an electronic catalog
    D. designing displays

21. The best way for a library media specialist to stay familiar and up-to-date with curriculum changes is to

    A. attend educational conferences
    B. serve on curriculum committees
    C. read professional journals in the major academic subject areas
    D. study commercial curriculum guides

22. Each of the following is a "core collection" selection tool for use in the library media center, EXCEPT

    A. *Children's Catalog*
    B. *The Elementary School Library Collection: A Guide to Books and Other Media*
    C. *Senior High School Library Catalog*
    D. *Media and Methods*

23. A library media specialist wants to link the school-based local area network (LAN) to a regional wide area network (WAN), in order to pool resources with other media centers. The fastest, highest-capacity technology available to enable reception of both voice and data over the same line at the same time would be

    A. digital subscriber lines (DSL)
    B. regular telephone lines with modems
    C. coaxial cable modems
    D. integrated services digital network (ISDN)

24. A library media staff creates multicopy order forms, and then creates their own files within their shelflist of the items on order. When such forms are used, the top copy is

    A. attached to the district office copy of the purchase order
    B. sent with the order
    C. filed under the purchase order number
    D. filed alphabetically under the author or title

25. Which of the following general library media periodicals is NOT available on-line? 25.____
    A. *Library Media Connection*
    B. *School Library Media Research*
    C. *School Library Journal*
    D. *School Library Media Activities Monthly*

KEY (CORRECT ANSWERS)

1. C
2. C
3. A
4. A
5. A

6. D
7. D
8. C
9. B
10. D

11. A
12. B
13. D
14. B
15. B

16. A
17. D
18. A
19. B
20. C

21. B
22. D
23. A
24. B
25. D

TEST 3

DIRECTIONS: Each question or incomplete statement is followed by several suggested answers or completions. Select the one the BEST answers the question or completes the statement. *PRINT THE LETTER OF THE CORRECT ANSWER IN THE SPACE AT THE RIGHT.*

1. The advantage of using OCR software with a scanner is that   1._____

    A. scanned files are compressed to save disk space
    B. scanned images can be saved and printed in their original color
    C. the software can scan photographs
    D. scanned files can be read by word processors

2. In general, preliminary budgets for a library media center should be prepared _____ in advance and shared with administrators for long-term planning.   2._____

    A. 6 months
    B. 1 year
    C. 2 years
    D. 3 years

3. Which of the following is NOT a fundamental principle that should guide the development of a library media center collection?   3._____

    A. Accessibility to timely, relevant information at both local and remote sites
    B. Consistency with local school board's adopted policies
    C. Selection from reputable reviewing tools or hands-on evaluation
    D. Selection of the largest collection possible under given space and budget restraints

4. Which of the following is an example of a call number from the Library of Congress classification system?   4._____

    A. As.345
    B. 987.765 Pe F476
    C. 694 Anderson
    D. GC111.2.M38

5. Library media specialists should establish collaborative partnerships with classroom teachers by   5._____
    I. accommodating planning/release time mandated for classroom teachers
    II. serving on curriculum development committees at all levels
    III. establishing the integration of information literacy skills across the curriculum
    IV. working jointly with teachers in planning, designing, teaching, and evaluating instructional activities

    A. I and II
    B. I, II and III
    C. II, III and IV
    D. I, II, III and IV

11

6. Which of the following is MOST likely to occur in the library media center as a result of the increased availability of electronic full-text access?

    A. Printed reference collections may become more generalized
    B. Space allotted for group work and activities may be reduced
    C. The need for periodical storage areas may diminish
    D. The need for supervision may diminish

7. A fourth-grade student is seeking news articles he can use to give a report on whales to the class. The most appropriate resource for this student is

    A. *Readers' Guide for Young People*
    B. Britannica.com
    C. *Readers' Guide to Periodical Literature*
    D. Lexis-Nexis

8. A library media specialist helps maintain a fully automated circulation system that makes use of the MARC format. Though the librarian is proficient in the MARC system, a new item arrives without documentation from the publisher about cataloging, and the specialist is unsure of how to catalog the item. The specialist should consult the

    A. American Library Association (ALA)
    B. Library of Congress
    C. *Sears List of Subject Headings*
    D. American Association of School Librarians (AASL)

9. The most significant advantage to the use of electronic reference software is

    A. the ease-of-use for teachers, regardless of authoring skills
    B. the inclusion of text, graphics, audio and video in one package
    C. its low up-front cost
    D. its suitability for all students, regardless of learning styles

10. During the next academic year, middle school teachers will conduct a new African literature course. No additional funds have been appropriated for print or nonprint resources for this course. The media specialist has already met with teachers and determined the resource needs. The most appropriate step to take next would be to

    A. request funds from the parent-teacher association
    B. submit a budget proposal to the principal
    C. apply for a grant
    D. solicit funds from local or state agencies

11. To a library media specialist, the term "digital divide" is a concept that refers to the issue of

    A. equity of access
    B. technology
    C. intellectual freedom
    D. confidentiality and privacy

12. The bottom portion of a call number in the Dewey system is usually an indication of the   12.____

    A. publication date
    B. subject
    C. author
    D. media type

13. The federal legislation that has done the most to direct public funding toward library media center collections has been the   13.____

    A. Civil Rights Act of 1964
    B. Elementary and Secondary Education Act of 1965
    C. Individuals with Disabilities Education Act of 1990
    D. No Child Left Behind Act of 2001

14. A library media specialist is filling out a budget request form for the purchase of several videotapes. The specialist first enters an account number to which the purchase will be charged, then the number, description, and total cost. Finally, the specialist fills in a column with the heading "Relation to plan" with the following entry: "Applies to year 2 of plan: to build video collection in curricular areas designated by English teachers." The type of budgeting system being used by the library media specialist is the _____ system.   14.____

    A. zero-based (ZBB)
    B. line-item
    C. program-planning-budgeting (PPBS)
    D. management by objectives (MBO)

15. A library media specialist marks items in the vertical file with a number, to facilitate circulation. The number usually consists of   15.____

    A. the year the item was added, followed by the accession number
    B. a call number based on the *Library of Congress Subject Headings*
    C. OCLC control number and the first three letters of the author's name
    D. the accession number only

16. Whether to use a jobber or a publisher for book orders is a decision that should be made on a case-to-case basis, keeping in mind that   16.____

    A. jobbers' supplies tend to fluctuate at different times of the year
    B. publishers often back-order items and delay shipments
    C. publishers do not offer discounts
    D. jobbers can offer books from a variety of publishers

17. Which of the following is a government-funded source of information that can be used to find suggestions for subject-specific and information skills curriculum?   17.____

    A. EBSCO
    B. Argus
    C. JSTOR
    D. ERIC

18. Of the following, which professional journal will most likely contain information about censorship cases in school library media centers?

    A. *Library Quarterly*
    B. *Booklist*
    C. *School Library Media Quarterly*
    D. *Newsletter on Intellectual Freedom*

19. The best way to establish priorities for a school library media program is through

    A. a study of best practices of library media specialists in comparable schools
    B. deliberations of a committee that represents the total school community
    C. an informal meeting with academic department chairs
    D. AASL guidelines

20. In designing a library media center, it should be generally calculated that _____ standard books will occupy one foot of shelving.

    A. 6
    B. 10
    C. 12
    D. 18

21. A library media specialist at a high school is considering the possibility of using student assistants to help with the daily tasks and procedures of the media center. In working with students, the specialist should adopt each of the following guidelines, EXCEPT

    A. compose a printed training manual that will be given to each assistant
    B. recruit assistants from among the students whose academic achievement is generally highest
    C. treat each assistantship as a real job, complete with posted requirements, a written application, recommendations, and an interview
    D. demonstrate the value of assistants with frequent rewards, recognition, and advancement

22. Of the following, the factor with the most significant effect on the overall environment of a library media center is the

    A. paint quality
    B. acoustics
    C. shelving layout
    D. ceiling surface

23. The Internet has changed reference services in a number of ways, both positive and negative. Positive effects include each of the following, EXCEPT

    A. greater likelihood of locating up-to-date information
    B. faster access to information
    C. access to a wider array of resources, such as government publications
    D. increased reliability of information

24. For creating an attractive flyer to promote a media center event, the most useful desktop publishing tool would be   24._____

    A. Pagemaker
    B. Autoformatting
    C. WordArt
    D. GUI

25. Together, an elementary math teacher and a library media specialist are designing a unit on reading and interpreting line and bar graphs. Which of the following would define a *performance task* included in this unit?   25._____

    A. Given a line or bar graph on paper or transparency, answer the following questions:
    B. Recognize that charts are graphs are representative
    C. Pinpoint the intersection and relationship between two factors
    D. Make a bar chart or line graph to represent the height of each person in your group

---

KEY (CORRECT ANSWERS)

1.	D		11.	A
2.	D		12.	C
3.	D		13.	B
4.	D		14.	C
5.	C		15.	A
6.	C		16.	D
7.	A		17.	D
8.	B		18.	D
9.	B		19.	B
10.	B		20.	B

21.	B
22.	B
23.	D
24.	C
25.	D

TEST 4

DIRECTIONS: Each question or incomplete statement is followed by several suggested answers or completions. Select the one the BEST answers the question or completes the statement. *PRINT THE LETTER OF THE CORRECT ANSWER IN THE SPACE AT THE RIGHT.*

1. Typically, the district's library media collection development/selection policy is   1._____

    A. a rough guideline open to interpretation by school library media specialists
    B. adopted without the input of school library media specialists
    C. a legally binding document
    D. the only body of rules necessary for a school library media center

2. Of the following, a library media program's ability to _____ is an appropriate standard   2._____
for measuring whether the number of staff employed in a library media program is adequate.

    A. maintain a staffing ratio of one media specialist for every 700 students
    B. assist students, teachers, and other patrons in areas of the school's instructional program
    C. provide individualized instruction to every student in the location of materials
    D. provide production services to teachers who want to edit multimedia presentations

3. A library media specialist at an elementary school is planning a renovation of the media   3._____
center, but has limited space. Which of the following areas could be most easily absorbed into other areas?

    A. Storytelling area
    B. Office(s)
    C. Workrooms and audiovisual areas
    D. Storage

4. When using on-line publications, a media specialist can archive information for later   4._____
retrieval by using a

    A. wizard
    B. Boolean search
    C. PDF file
    D. bookmark or favorite

5. The principal advantage associated with computer networking in a library media center is   5._____

    A. privacy and security
    B. firewalls and other software utility tools
    C. standardization of hardware and public access
    D. shared hardware and software tools and resources

6. The most important reason for a library media specialist to evaluate and revise an   6._____
instructional activity is to

    A. achieve a final format that requires no further revision
    B. ensure that the lesson can be delivered within a given time frame

C. obtain favorable student evaluations
D. improve the activity's effectiveness

7. The ALA's *Information Power* charges the library media specialist with four distinct roles. Which of the following is NOT one of them?

    A. Instructional consultant
    B. Advocate
    C. Teacher
    D. Information specialist

8. A library user is looking for information on the recent history, government, and economy of Afghanistan. The best resource for this inquiry would be the

    A. Lexis-Nexis Information Service
    B. *CIA World Factbook*
    C. Ebsco Information Services
    D. A World Atlas

9. Which of the following standardized sources for subject cataloging is most likely to be used by a library media specialist at a middle school?

    A. *Sears List of Subject Headings*
    B. *Subject Headings for Children: A List of Subject Headings Used by the Library of Congress with Dewey Numbers*
    C. *Library of Congress Subject Headings*
    D. *Anglo-American Cataloging Rules (AACR2)*

10. Several studies conducted in the last two decades have suggested that the strongest predictor of test performance for young children is

    A. the size of library print collections
    B. school library media center expenditures
    C. degree of collaboration between teachers and library media specialists
    D. family socioeconomic status

11. General guidelines exist to define the life cycles of library media center materials and to estimate budget considerations. For non-fiction print titles, the recommended guideline is a life cycle of _____ years.

    A. 4
    B. 8
    C. 12
    D. 18

12. Historically, most court cases involving libraries have centered on the issue of

    A. accreditation
    B. privacy
    C. copyright
    D. First Amendment rights

13. Many library media specialists rely on reviews in professional periodicals to help them make decisions about purchases. Which of the following statements about such reviews is FALSE?

    A. They are seldom written by practitioners who regularly analyze materials for their own collection
    B. They only review about 25 percent of the materials published.
    C. They are generally not useful for making judgements about specific library communities or how a material will fit in with a certain curriculum.
    D. They review very few small-press releases.

14. A library media specialist is composing the media center's annual report. Most likely, the main body of the report will begin with

    A. cumulated statistics and analysis
    B. a statement of the media center's positive accomplishments
    C. a description of projects
    D. goals for the coming year

15. In a 1973 lawsuit that was eventually settled by both CBS and Vanderbilt University, the university was granted the right to copy and archive

    A. documentary programs
    B. talk shows
    C. news broadcasts
    D. educational programs

16. A library media specialist is filling out an order form to a book jobber. The specialist is worried about spending all his book/periodicals budget within the budgetary time limit. He should

    A. submit both a main order and a supplemental order to fill in for back-orders
    B. specify "absolutely no back orders"
    C. specify that this is a "rush" order
    D. try to contact the publishers of the items directly

17. A high school student is researching a presentation on immigration reform at both the national level and in her own state. The most appropriate Internet directory resource for this student would be

    A. Lexis-Nexis
    B. FindLaw
    C. Britannica.com
    D. Beaucoup

18. In the school library media center budgeting process, any purchase billed so that it does not clear the system by _____ is typically charged to the next year's budget.

    A. May 15
    B. July 1
    C. September 30
    D. December 15

19. A library media specialist at a middle school is working to tailor the media center's program to fit the school's instructional methods. As he goes through this process, the specialist should keep in mind that on the whole, middle school students benefit from an instructional program that focuses on

    A. applying already developed skills in problem-solving situations
    B. varying both the content and the skills that are demanded of students
    C. relating one body of knowledge to another
    D. primary drill and practice

19.____

20. Which of the following is an electronic discussion group that serves the school library community?

    A. Library Talk
    B. ICONnect
    C. Continuing Library Education Network and Exchange (CLENERT)
    D. LM_NET

20.____

21. In terms of its quality and consistency in reaching stated goals and objectives, evaluation of the library media center is useful for
    I. providing a rationale for expenditures
    II. conducting focus group interviews
    III. developing a long-range plan
    IV. evaluating written goals and developing new ones

    A. I only
    B. I, II and III
    C. III and IV
    D. I, II, III and IV

21.____

22. The appropriate book-stack shelving height for middle-school students is _____ inches.

    A. 42
    B. 60
    C. 72
    D. 96

22.____

23. The best strategy for locating *Sense and Sensibility* is to search for the title in

    A. a poetry index
    B. a periodical index
    C. the card catalog
    D. a reference book

23.____

24. A library media specialist has recently updated the reference collection at a high school library, and wants to acquaint students with the new materials. The most effective way to do this is to

    A. prominently display the new materials in the library media center
    B. place an advertisement about the new materials in the school newsletter
    C. with teachers, plan activities that will encourage the use of the new materials
    D. distribute lists of the new materials to the students

24.____

25. Most school-based local area networks (LANs) are a group of computers connected by cabling to a(n) _____ and peripherals such as printers.   25.___

    A. file server
    B. telecommunications network
    C. Internet service provider (ISP)
    D. network interface card (NIC)

KEY (CORRECT ANSWERS)

1.	C	11.	C
2.	B	12.	D
3.	A	13.	A
4.	D	14.	A
5.	D	15.	C
6.	D	16.	A
7.	B	17.	B
8.	B	18.	B
9.	A	19.	B
10.	B	20.	D

21. C
22. B
23. C
24. C
25. A

EXAMINATION SECTION
TEST 1

DIRECTIONS: Each question or incomplete statement is followed by several suggested answers or completions. Select the one that BEST answers the question or completes the statement. *PRINT THE LETTER OF THE CORRECT ANSWER IN THE SPACE AT THE RIGHT.*

1. Which of the following is LEAST likely to be included in an accession record? 1._____

    A. Source
    B. Budgetary fund
    C. Accession number
    D. Price paid

2. A user is seeking popular information about recent political events in the United States. Which of the following indexes should be used? 2._____

    A. *Social Science Index*
    B. *MLA International Bibliography*
    C. *Lexis-Nexis Academic*
    D. *EBSCO Military and Government*

3. Which of the following is NOT a Boolean search term? 3._____

    A. AND
    B. NOT
    C. IF
    D. OR

4. A field in a MARC record is tagged "910." The field contains data 4._____

    A. about the edition
    B. of local interest
    C. for control purposes
    D. about the title

5. In _____ indexing, an algorithm is applied by a computer to the title and/or text of a work to identify and extract words and phrases representing subjects. 5._____

    A. assignment
    B. derivative
    C. automatic
    D. string

6. Most books and periodical articles receive more than one subject heading because 6._____
    I. the more headings a book or article receives, the more chances a searcher has to locate it
    II. most books and articles cover more than one subject
    III. this is a task for which most libraries are notoriously over staffed
    IV. they are classified by more than one person, on more than one occasion

    A. I only   B. I and II   C. II only   D. II, III and IV

21

7. The National Media Library defines two types of storage environments in digital libraries: access storage and archive storage. Which of the following statements is TRUE?

   A. Access storage has a humidity requirement significantly lower than archival storage.
   B. Archival storage involves a significantly lower temperature set point than access storage.
   C. Archival storage ensures a much longer media life expectancy.
   D. The conditions of access storage don't always allow immediate access or playback.

8. After deciding to offer users online access to an electronic journals collection through the library's online catalog, a library must decide whether to use the "single-record" or "separate-record" approach to offering access to print and electronic versions. Which of the following statements is FALSE?

   A. The separate-record approach is preferred when the online version has significant additional content not present in the original.
   B. The separate-record approach generally offers less expensive, faster access.
   C. The single-record approach is considered MOST valid when the online version contains sufficient full text to be a good substitute, and contains no significant additional content.
   D. The single-record approach is commonly applied when the online version lacks full test or has only full text from the original, and is therefore not considered to be an adequate substitute.

9. In the Library of Congress classification, numbers that begin with L are typically associated with

   A. music
   B. physical science
   C. law
   D. education

10. The trend toward outsourcing library services has proved beneficial for the bottom line of many libraries. In general, however, the outsourcing of _____ has proven to be the most controversial for libraries.

    A. conservation and preservation
    B. acquisitions plans
    C. cataloging and selection
    D. physical processing

11. In _____ level cataloging, an encoding level developed for use in the Program for Cooperative Cataloging (PCC), fields of fixed length are fully coded, but a list of exceptions applies to certain fields of variable length.

    A. full   B. core
    C. minimal   D. collection

12. In a markup language such as HTML, the basic units of information are known as   12.____

    A. entities
    B. items
    C. elements
    D. fields

13. Speed of transmission over a network is sometimes negatively affected by applications   13.____
    such as "bandwidth hogs." Which of the following type of file is LEAST likely to compromise the transmission speed of a network?

    A. RealAudio
    B. MP3
    C. PDF
    D. Windows Media

14. Potential library uses for computer workstations include   14.____
    I. Internet access tool
    II. management/administrative tool
    III. interlibrary loan management
    IV. collection control

    A. I and II
    B. I, II and III
    C. II and III
    D. I, II, III and IV

15. A search of a database containing 100 records relevant to a topic retrieves 75 records,   15.____
    25 of which are relevant to the topic. The search is said to have _____ percent precision, or relevance ratio.

    A. 25
    B. 33
    C. 50
    D. 75

16. A typical use of JavaScript is to   16.____

    A. developing the user interface at the server side
    B. execute instructions written in a high-level language
    C. store Java application for use on a single workstation, for use in any online activity initiated by the user
    D. check data that a user provides as input as soon as it has been typed, rather than transmit it back to the server for validation

17. The TIFF and JPEG standards for representing digital images, while in many ways superior to the GIF format, present challenges in association with   17.____

    A. accessibility
    B. platform independence
    C. resolution
    D. preservation

18. In library cataloging, _____ are used to indicate interpolation, and to enclose the general material designation that follows the title in a bibliographic record that represents a nonbook item.

    A. parentheses
    B. square brackets
    C. italics
    D. bold letters

19. To locate appropriate subject headings for a preliminary search, patrons should use

    A. EBSCO Information Services
    B. the ERIC *Thesaurus*
    C. an abstract journal
    D. *Library of Congress Subject Headings*

20. Which of the following is an advantage associated with the "film-first" approach to preservation-in which microfilm records are later scanned to produce digital records?

    A. Excellent quality maintenance over generations of analog reproduction
    B. High-resolution photographic process
    C. Opportunity for image enhancement during image capture
    D. High dynamic range for complex images

21. The weeding policies of most public libraries are based on the criterion of

    A. usage
    B. content
    C. subject area
    D. date of publication

22. When making use of interlibrary loan services, a user must typically have done each of the following, EXCEPT

    A. provided bibliographic information
    B. requested a specific title
    C. seen the material to be borrowed
    D. provided references to citations of the materials

23. Which of the following is an electronic bibliographic utility?

    A. *GOBI*   B. *ProQuest*
    C. *OCLC*   D. *ODLIS*

24. The criteria for the modes of access a library is willing to accept and support is one of the most important parts of an electronic journal collection policy. The library will typically need to develop a stance on _____ as part of these criteria.

    I. simultaneous use
    II. user definition
    III. subject parameters
    IV. comprehensiveness of full text

    A. I and II
    B. I, II and IV
    C. II, III and IV
    D. I, II, III and IV

25. The Children's Internet Protection Act of 2000
    I. pegged the government-mandated discount on Internet access to compliance with certain filtering practices
    II. provided funds for libraries to implement filtering
    III. established local control over Internet access
    IV. was ruled unconstitutional by the Supreme Court.

    A. I and II
    B. II only
    C. II, III and IV
    D. I, II, III and IV

KEY (CORRECT ANSWERS)

1. B	6. B	11. B	16. D	21. A
2. C	7. B	12. A	17. D	22. C
3. C	8. B	13. C	18. B	23. C
4. B	9. D	14. D	19. D	24. A
5. C	10. C	15. B	20. B	25. A

TEST 2

DIRECTIONS: Each question or incomplete statement is followed by several suggested answers or completions. Select the one that BEST answers the question or completes the statement. *PRINT THE LETTER OF THE CORRECT ANSWER IN THE SPACE AT THE RIGHT.*

1. In cataloging, the purpose of a scope note is to   1.____

   A. indicate that a term is used as a subheading under one or more categories of headings
   B. direct a cataloger to classify works in multiple locations
   C. instruct a Dewey Decimal cataloger to append to a given base number one or more numbers found elsewhere in the classification, in order to build a class number
   D. indicate the intended use or meaning of a term in an indexing language, and any special rules for assigning it in indexing.

2. The imprint of a book includes the   2.____

   A. printing history
   B. editor's name
   C. edition of the book
   D. publisher's name

3. Which of the following is NOT an electronic periodical reference tool?   3.____

   A. *InfoTrac*
   B. *ProQuest*
   C. *EBSCOhost*
   D. *GOBI*

4. The first part of a full URL designates a   4.____

   A. protocol
   B. domain name
   C. file
   D. port

5. The FIRST step in writing a library's technology plan is typically to   5.____

   A. investigate existing options and opportunities
   B. conduct a needs assessment
   C. create a budget
   D. inventory the current technology

6. In electronic journal publishing, vendor gateways may offer   6.____
   I. a single interface for browsing journals from different publishers
   II. alerting services
   III. an electronic archive for selected titles
   IV. management reports for collection development and budgeting

   A. I only   B. I and II
   C. I, III and IV   D. I, II, III and IV

7. Which of the following electronic discussion groups focuses on school librarians and school library issues?

    A. *SYSLIB-L*
    B. *Web4Lib*
    C. *LIBSOFT*
    D. *LM_NET*

8. Each of the following is a listserv designed to announce the online availability of new journals, EXCEPT

    A. Highwire Press
    B. Fulltext Sources Online
    C. ECO
    D. Catchword

9. The _____ fields in the MARC system contain control information, numbers, and codes.

    A. OXX
    B. 1XX
    C. 5XX
    D. 8XX

10. In Internet user, instead of being taken to a desired Web page, instead is taken to a page that says *Error Message 400*. What has happened?

    A. A password has been set up on the server for access.
    B. The file has been moved or deleted, or the URL in incorrect.
    C. Special permission is needed to access the site.
    D. The syntax used in the URL is incorrect.

11. What is the term for an electronic database that is used to translate between different representations of geospatial references-such as place names and geographic coordinates?

    A. Atlas
    B. Gazetteer
    C. GPS
    D. Mapquest

12. In the library literature, materials designated with the collecting level "1" in relation to a given subject are considered

    A. "out of scope"
    B. useful as a comprehensive resource
    C. useful as a source of minimal information
    D. a potential resource for study or instructional support

13. ANSI/NISO standards for abstracting specify that each of the following should be used in writing an abstract, EXCEPT

    A. definitions
    B. the past tense
    C. background of a study
    D. articles and conjunctions

14. In a searchable online database, a user types the following term: *children and violence and ((television or media) not cartoon)*. The use of parentheses is an example of the technique known as

    A. expansion
    B. truncation
    C. stringing
    D. nesting

15. Each of the following is an advantage associated with searching for information online, EXCEPT that

    A. users can combine search terms
    B. the information is usually more accurate than in print sources
    C. the information is updated more frequently
    D. online searches are usually faster

16. The principal advantage associated with the use of hard disk drives for digital information storage is that they

    A. are formatted into tracks and sectors
    B. don't use the binder/substrate structure that can limit physical longevity
    C. use more than one laser
    D. offer rapid, direct access to information

17. _____ rights are granted for the reprinting of a work in its entirety in an anthology

    A. Volume
    B. Serial
    C. First
    D. Subsidiary

18. Subject encyclopedias are well-suited to undergraduate research because

    A. they have been endorsed by experts in the field
    B. their articles are written by laypersons
    C. they offer broad knowledge that serves as a solid initial encounter with knowledge
    D. they often provide bibliographies to additional sources

19. What is the term for a text file on a computer that stores personal preferences used by a specific server?

    A. Cookie
    B. Applet
    C. Bot
    D. Proxy

20. In book sales, the typical library discount is _____ percent.

    A. 1-5
    B. 5-10
    C. 15-25
    D. 30-45

21. An article is cited from a well-known reference book using the MLA format. Which of the following, even if known, is LEAST likely to be included in the citation?

    A. Publisher
    B. Author
    C. Date of publication
    D. Title of article

22. In _____ indexing, a set of indexing terms is assigned to a document by a human indexer, and then the terms are manipulated by computer to create an index in which each term is listed in correct alphabetical sequence, providing access to the document under each of the terms.

    A. string
    B. automatic
    C. pre-coordinate
    D. derivative

23. Which of the following MARC tags is NOT frequently used in cataloging books?

    A. 010
    B. 246
    C. 480
    D. 651

24. A measure of the effectiveness of information retrieval, computed as the ratio of nonrelevant entries or items retrieved in response to a query to the total number of nonrelevant items indexed in the database, is

    A. fallout
    B. recall
    C. false drops
    D. precision

25. The Library of Congress subject heading "Forests and forestry" is an example of a(n) _____ indexing term.

    A. aggregate
    B. hierarchical
    C. unitary
    D. associative

KEY (CORRECT ANSWERS)

1. D	6. D	11. B	16. D	21. A
2. D	7. D	12. C	17. A	22. A
3. D	8. B	13. C	18. D	23. C
4. A	9. A	14. D	19. A	24. A
5. D	10. D	15. B	20. B	25. C

EXAMINATION SECTION
TEST 1

DIRECTIONS: Each question or incomplete statement is followed by several suggested answers or completions. Select the one that BEST answers the question or completes the statement. *PRINT THE LETTER OF THE CORRECT ANSWER IN THE SPACE AT THE RIGHT.*

1. A library is in the process of conducting an annual performance evaluation. Which of the following would be an output measure that might be used in this process? 1.____

   A. Staff expenditures
   B. User satisfaction survey results
   C. Ratio of computer workstations to daily average users
   D. Ratio of interlibrary loan lending to borrowing

2. The _____ record is a separate record attached to the bibliographic record for a serial title in which the receipt of individual issues or parts is entered on an ongoing basis. 2.____

   A. holdings
   B. check-in
   C. item
   D. periodical

3. Of the following, which research tool would be most appropriate for finding where an author uses specific words or phrases? 3.____

   A. Abstract
   B. Gazetteer
   C. Dictionary
   D. Concordance

4. In library cataloging, a separately published part of a bibliographic resource, usually representing a subject category within the whole and indicated by a topical heading or an alphanumeric heading, is a(n) 4.____

   A. class
   B. scope
   C. notch
   D. section

5. The main advantage to paying an electronic journal publisher on a per-article basis, rather than subscribing to a package or database, is that 5.____

   A. hardware, browser, and networking requirements are simpler
   B. the library pays only for what it uses
   C. costs are shifted entirely to the user
   D. costs are more predictable over time

6. The Dublin Core Metadata Initiative, an international effort to develop standard mechanisms for searching online resources, has named 15 core metadata elements to be used to direct searches. Which of the following is NOT one of these? 6.____

   A. Editor   B. Rights   C. Date   D. Format

7. "Converting" electronic records means that

   A. there is a change to the underlying bit stream, but there is no change in the representation or intellectual content of the records
   B. they are moved from a proprietary legacy system that lacks software functionality to an open system
   C. they have been transferred from old storage media to new storage media with the same format specifications and without any loss in structure, content, or context
   D. they have been exported or imported from one software environment to another without the loss of structure, content, or context even though the underlying bit stream has likely been altered

8. The 3XX fields in the MARC system contain

   A. physical descriptions
   B. main entries
   C. subject added entries
   D. titles, editions, and imprints

9. In Internet user, instead of being taken to a desired Web page, instead is taken to a page that says *Error Message 404*. What has happened?

   A. Either the server is busy, or the site has moved.
   B. Special permission is needed to access the site.
   C. The file has been moved or deleted, or the URL in incorrect.
   D. The syntax used in the URL is incorrect.

10. An anthology is compiled by 6 authors. According to the MLA format, how many of the author's names should be included in a citation?

    A. 0
    B. 1
    C. 2
    D. 6

11. Which of the following is NOT an advantage of using HTML as a format for file preservation?

    A. Extensive authoring tools
    B. Improving tools for conversion-to-HTML
    C. Good standard for delivering simple text
    D. Can be viewed in any browser

12. In the MARC record, the same digits are assigned across fields in the second and third character positions of the tag to indicate data of the same type. For example, tags reading "X10" contain information about

    A. topical terms   B. bibliographic titles
    C. uniform titles   D. corporate names

13. A librarian wants to subscribe to an e-mail newsletter that contains annotations of information technology articles and other items written by a team of librarians and library staff. She is wary, however, of having her inbox clogged with unread material that arrives too frequently for her to read it all, and would prefer to have the newsletter arrive monthly. The librarian should subscribe to

    A. *Free Pint*
    B. *Edupage*
    C. *Current Cites*
    D. *NewsScan*

14. A journal's "impact factor," a measure of its relative importance, is most often defined as the _____ in a given year.

    A. number of electronic queries coming from a library database
    B. frequency of citations to its articles
    C. number of top-rated professionals or scholars who publish in it
    D. times the full-text is displayed on a library terminal

15. _____ is the online database designed and maintained since 1995 by the Library of Congress to make legislative information accessible to the public

    A. CQ
    B. NARA
    C. THOMAS
    D. FindLaw

16. The main software protocol that manages data on the Internet is

    A. TCP/IP
    B. HTTP
    C. HTML
    D. FTP

17. Which of the following is a repeatable MARC field?

    A. 100
    B. 246
    C. 250
    D. 260

18. A user seeking articles about transportation should be directed to Wilson's _____ Index.

    A. Social Sciences
    B. Business Periodicals
    C. Applied Science and Technology
    D. General Science

19. In the library literature, materials designated with the collecting level "4" in relation to a given subject are considered

    A. "out of scope"
    B. sources of basic information
    C. comprehensive and authoritative
    D. useful for the support of research in the given subject

20. In Web addresses, the hashmark is used to

    A. create a link to another location in the same document
    B. identify a port
    C. create a link to another Web page
    D. differentiate numerical characters

21. The content of a Web site is difficult to navigate, and users tend to get confused when trying to find information. The resource assessment guideline that needs to be addressed is

    A. Documentation and Credibility
    B. Ease of Use, Navigation, and Accessibility
    C. User Interface and Design
    D. Content

22. To extend the accessibility of any material that can be displayed at a library workstation to those with extremely poor vision, _____ can be used.

    A. screen reading software
    B. screen magnifying software
    C. TTY
    D. an on-screen keyboard

23. The software application needed to read files in Portable Document Format (PDF) is known as

    A. Acrobat Reader
    B. Real Page
    C. Pagemaker
    D. techexplorer Hypermedia Browser

24. In data that is prepared in the cataloging-in-publication (CIP) format and distributed in MARC format prior to a work's publication, the element that typically appears after the notes about bibliographical references or previous editions is the

    A. Library of Congress classification number
    B. statement of responsibility
    C. ISBN
    D. Dewey Decimal classification number

25. The reason for the slow pace of initial acceptance of WORM (write once, read many) technology in library archiving is that 25.____
    A. the amount of storage available on the disks is too variable to offer predictable capacity
    B. disks are not standardized and can be read only on the type of drive used to write them
    C. the data cannot be altered once it is stored
    D. the longevity of the disk media is still unknown

KEY (CORRECT ANSWERS)

1. D	6. A	11. A	16. A	21. B
2. B	7. D	12. D	17. B	22. A
3. D	8. A	13. C	18. C	23. A
4. D	9. C	14. B	19. D	24. C
5. B	10. B	15. C	20. A	25. B

TEST 2

DIRECTIONS: Each question or incomplete statement is followed by several suggested answers or completions. Select the one that BEST answers the question or completes the statement. *PRINT THE LETTER OF THE CORRECT ANSWER IN THE SPACE AT THE RIGHT.*

1. Which of the following is NOT an aggregator service? 1.____

   A. ScienceDirect
   B. JSTOR
   C. Britannica
   D. Blackwell's Electronic Journal Navigator

2. Technical service librarians are usually concerned with any of the following, EXCEPT 2.____

   A. repairing damaged materials
   B. checking in journals
   C. cataloging books
   D. checking books out

3. Materials that are published electronically are identified by their 3.____

   A. EAD
   B. DOI
   C. XLS
   D. ISBN

4. Which of the following is an example of "mobile code" that allows a Web designer to incorporate computer programs, such as Flash pages, into Web page content? 4.____

   A. Packet
   B. Worm
   C. Warez
   D. Applet

5. The abbreviation "NOP" on a publisher's invoice usually means the requested item 5.____

   A. is on back order
   B. is not in print
   C. the requested item is not published by the vendor
   D. has not yet been published, but will be in the future

6. A well-designed online catalog or bibliographic database allows the user to employ limiting parameters to restrict the retrieval or entries including the terms included in the search statement. Which of the following is NOT a common example of these "limiters?" 6.____

   A. Spelling
   B. Publication date
   C. Full-text
   D. Locally held

7. Which of the following is LEAST likely to be a guideline followed in setting up an electronic reserves (ER) system in an academic library?

   A. Restrict access to authorized users off-site, but maintain open access on-site.
   B. Limit offsite access by course and/or instructor name.
   C. Remove or suppress access at the end of every session.
   D. Post copyright warning notices.

8. Subsystems of the Internet include
   I. the World Wide Web
   II. Newsgroups
   III. Telnet
   IV. e-mail

   A. I only
   B. I, II and III
   C. II and III
   D. I, II, III and IV

9. Binary scanning at 300 dots per inch (dpi) is usually considered adequate for

   A. halftones
   B. illustrated text
   C. typed or laser-printed archival documents
   D. published text/line art

10. The systems librarian's responsibilities typically include each of the following, EXCEPT

    A. development and maintenance of hardware and software
    B. Webmaster
    C. training staff in the use of library systems
    D. interlibrary loan processing

11. A records survey is LEAST likely to be used for the purpose of determining the _____ of archival records.

    A. quality
    B. content
    C. physical quantities
    D. provenance

12. In the searching of an electronic database, which of the following might cause a "false drop?"

    A. The omission of older information
    B. Too-frequent updating of the database
    C. A word with more than one meaning
    D. Restrictions on database use

13. A group of librarians is meeting to determine the selection of electronic journals for a library's collection. One of the MOST likely disadvantages of including the reference librarian in this group is that he may not

    A. have close contact with users
    B. be accustomed to the collaborative approach
    C. be able to relinquish his primary responsibilities for long enough periods of time
    D. have experience selecting and supporting electronic resources

14. Most Internet service providers (ISPs) are built on _____ lines.

    A. 56 Kbps
    B. ISDN
    C. T-1
    D. T-3

15. Which of the following is a term used to denote a hard copy enlargement of an image on microform?

    A. Blowback
    B. Macroform
    C. Aperture card
    D. Blowup

16. On the Web or in an online bibliography, well-designed search software is capable of
    I. searching more than one database simultaneously
    II. removing duplicate record s from results when searching multiple databases
    III. viewing search terms highlighted in results
    IV. printing, e-mailing, and downloading results in various formats

    A. I only
    B. I and III
    C. III only
    D. I, II, III and IV

17. Subject heading systems do NOT

    A. assist searchers in understanding how a specific subject fits into a larger structure of knowledge
    B. divide knowledge over 30 broad categories
    C. describe what a book or article is about
    D. allow people to search by subject area

18. In order to ensure the integrity of digital archive, the origin and chain of custody of a particular file or record most be preserved. This feature of information integrity is known as

    A. content
    B. provenance
    C. content
    D. fixity

19. The creation of a Web page could involve
    I. using a dedicated Web authoring software program
    II. converting a word-processed document to HTML
    III. converting a magazine article, with images, to PDF
    IV. use the Web authoring capability of a portal

    A. I and II
    B. I, II and IV
    C. II and III
    D. II, III and IV

20. What is the general term for an indexable concept that is assigned to add depth to subject indexing, and that is not listed in the thesaurus of indexing terms because it either represents a proper name or a concept that is not yet authorized for inclusion in the bibliographic database?

    A. assigner
    B. identifier
    C. descriptor
    D. ideogram

21. The *World of Learning* is an example of a(n)

    A. concordance
    B. encyclopedia
    C. abstract
    D. directory

22. In the United States, the professional association for academic libraries and librarians is the

    A. Association of College and Research Libraries (ACRL)
    B. Association of Specialized and Cooperative Library Agencies (ASCLA)
    C. American Library Association (ALA)
    D. National Commission on Libraries and Information Science (NCLIS)

23. The module of the library automation system that is used by the public for interacting with the system is the

    A. circulation module
    B. serials module
    C. OPAC
    D. cataloging module

24. Which of the following is a synthetic classification system?

    A. Dewey Decimal
    B. Colon classification
    C. Library of Congress classification
    D. Sears List

25. Library issues concerning the USA Patriot Act include
    I. civil liberties related to privacy and confidentiality
    II. denial of access to information
    III. fair use
    IV. copyright law

    A. I and II
    B. II only
    C. II, III and IV
    D. I, II, III and IV

25.___

KEY (CORRECT ANSWERS)

1. C	6. A	11. A	16. D	21. D
2. D	7. A	12. C	17. B	22. A
3. B	8. D	13. C	18. B	23. C
4. D	9. C	14. C	19. B	24. B
5. C	10. D	15. A	20. B	25. A

EXAMINATION SECTION
TEST 1

DIRECTIONS: Each question or incomplete statement is followed by several suggested answers or completions. Select the one that BEST answers the question or completes the statement. *PRINT THE LETTER OF THE CORRECT ANSWER IN THE SPACE AT THE RIGHT.*

1. The BEST known encyclopedia in the Western world, first published in the 18th century, was 1.____

   A. WORLD BOOK ENCYCLOPEDIA
   B. COMPTON'S PICTURED ENCYCLOPEDIA
   C. ENCYCLOPEDIA BRITANNICA
   D. ENCYCLOPEDIA AMERICANA

2. Authority-control records are important in an online catalog environment because they 2.____

   A. help prevent *blind* cross-references
   B. expand the capacity of the database
   C. keep the system from overloading
   D. provide access to fugitive materials

3. Which of the following is NOT the name of an online catalog? 3.____

   A. Geobase   B. Dynix   C. Geac   D. OCLC

4. Nom de plume is synonymous with 4.____

   A. pseudonym   B. nickname
   C. given name   D. telonism

5. Component-word searching is another way of saying _____ searching. 5.____

   A. key-word   B. permuterm
   C. subject   D. author/title

6. The citation indexes (SCIENCE CITATION INDEX, etc.) are unique in that they 6.____

   A. allow searching by the name of an institution
   B. provide access to foreign language journals
   C. allow searching of an author's references
   D. contain millions of unique records

7. A good online public access catalog (OPAC) can be expected to provide all of the following EXCEPT 7.____

   A. author and title access to books and audio-visual materials
   B. the loan status of materials that circulate
   C. information regarding who a book has been loaned to
   D. the place and publisher of each book in the catalog

8. Of the points to consider in a systematic evaluation of an encyclopedia, the LEAST important one is 8.____

   A. cost   B. viewpoint and objectivity
   C. subject coverage   D. number of pages

9. Widespread searching of bibliographic databases dates back to

   A. the 1950's B. 1960
   C. the mid-1980's D. the early 1970's

10. The format of a reference set means the

    A. writing style
    B. binding and size
    C. authority of contributors
    D. viewpoint and objectivity

11. The FIRST bibliographic databases were by-products of

    A. progress in NASA technology
    B. online card catalogs such as OCLC
    C. information dissemination centers
    D. the computerized typesetting operation

12. A patron asks your advice as a librarian on a set of encyclopedias he is considering for his family.
    The MOST helpful response for you is to

    A. give limited advice and provide the patron with professional reviews of the set under question
    B. give no advice for fear of repercussions from sales-persons and publishers
    C. endorse or condemn the set whole-heartedly, depending on your own opinion
    D. refer the patron to the director of the library

13. The four basic components of the online industry include all of the following EXCEPT

    A. libraries and information centers
    B. library school administrators
    C. end-users who request information
    D. database producers

14. McGraw-Hill's ENCYCLOPEDIA OF WORLD ART is an example of a _____ encyclopedia.

    A. children's B. subject
    C. supermarket D. foreign

15. Which of the following bibliographic databases is NOT produced by a federal government agency or federally-supported institution?

    A. ERIC B. COMPENDEX C. AGRICOLA D. MEDLINE

16. A ready-reference work is one which

    A. is allowed to circulate outside of the library
    B. is especially difficult to use
    C. arrives on a monthly basis
    D. is useful for *quick* questions of a factual nature

17. All of the following are examples of source documents EXCEPT

    A. patents
    B. conference papers
    C. indexes
    D. newspapers

18. The STATISTICAL ABSTRACT OF THE UNITED STATES is a compendium in the sense that it

    A. contains statistics on a wide range of subjects
    B. is published on an annual basis
    C. is a summary of U.S. Census data
    D. can be used for research in education

19. The number EJ121478, as part of an ERIC record, would indicate that the material referenced

    A. is a journal article
    B. is a book
    C. is an ERIC document on microfiche
    D. was entered in the database in 1978

20. A thesaurus which accompanies an index such as ERIC is a list of

    A. corporate authors
    B. journals indexed
    C. stop words
    D. assigned descriptors

KEY (CORRECT ANSWERS)

1.	C		11.	D
2.	A		12.	A
3.	A		13.	B
4.	A		14.	B
5.	A		15.	B
6.	C		16.	D
7.	C		17.	C
8.	D		18.	C
9.	D		19.	A
10.	B		20.	D

TEST 2

DIRECTIONS: Each question or incomplete statement is followed by several suggested answers or completions. Select the one that BEST answers the question or completes the statement. *PRINT THE LETTER OF THE CORRECT ANSWER IN THE SPACE AT THE RIGHT.*

1. The U.S. National Library of Medicine produces all of the following databases EXCEPT   1.____

    A. EMBASE   B. AIDSLINE   C. CANCERLIT   D. MEDLINE

2. H.W. Wilson's CURRENT BIOGRAPHY provides   2.____

    A. essay-length biographical information
    B. reference to information in BIOGRAPHY INDEX
    C. no more information on an individual than is provided by WHO'S WHO
    D. reviews of best-selling biographies

3. The database which provides access to fugitive materials in education is   3.____

    A. Academic Index
    B. Education Index
    C. ERIC
    D. Mental Measurements Yearbook

4. All of the following are covered in CONTEMPORARY AUTHORS EXCEPT   4.____

    A. screenwriters   B. poets
    C. dramatists   D. technical writers

5. Boolean logic utilizes all of the following logical operators EXCEPT   5.____

    A. if   B. or   C. not   D. and

6. A prescriptive dictionary is one which   6.____

    A. discusses in great detail the origin of a word
    B. adheres to tradition and historical authority for word definitions and approved usage
    C. attempts to relate every possible definition and usage of a word
    D. is published only in the United States

7. Free-text searching in a bibliographic database means   7.____

    A. searching several descriptors at one time
    B. using Boolean logic in your search
    C. searching without the use of controlled vocabulary
    D. searching only titles and abstracts

8. ABRIDGED INDEX MEDICUS differs from INDEX MEDICUS in that it   8.____

    A. contains citations to English-language journals only
    B. contains only information from the last twelve months
    C. contains citations to foreign-language journals only
    D. is not published by the National Library of Medicine

9. The two PRINCIPAL operations of public services are

    A. circulation and reference
    B. reference and serials management
    C. circulation and collection development
    D. reference and classification

10. Of the following reasons for an academic library to acquire the DICTIONARY OF AMERICAN SLANG, which is the LEAST valid?

    A. Most regular dictionaries do not indicate the variations of meaning of given slang terms or words.
    B. Students often come across expressions which are not defined well in ordinary dictionaries.
    C. It is a good source to check on the language used by an author to convey a character's background or social class.
    D. Students and librarians alike enjoy reading through it during their leisure time.

11. Collection maintenance includes all of the following EXCEPT

    A. taking inventory   B. reshelving books
    C. identifying overdues   D. shelf-reading

12. A gazetteer is a

    A. biographical dictionary
    B. good source for looking up phases of the moon
    C. geographical dictionary
    D. guide to motels throughout the United States

13. A Dewey Decimal Classification number never has MORE than how many digits to the LEFT of the decimal?

    A. Four   B. Five   C. Three   D. Two

14. In MOST government depository libraries, the government documents are arranged on the shelves

    A. by Superintendent of Documents numbers
    B. by Library of Congress call numbers
    C. by Dewey Decimal numbers
    D. alphabetically by title

15. The Library of Congress Classification System is different from the Dewey Decimal Classification System in that it

    A. arranges books on the shelf by subject
    B. does not include author numbers
    C. is not frequently used by libraries in the United States
    D. was developed to meet the needs of a specific library's collection

3 (#2)

16. The BEST reference source for finding, in detail, the organization and activities of all U.S. government agencies is

    A. POLITICS IN AMERICA
    B. THE STATESMAN'S YEARBOOK
    C. UNITED STATES GOVERNMENT MANUAL
    D. MOODY'S MUNICIPAL AND GOVERNMENT MANUAL

17. The added entries in a catalog record could be for

    A. joint authors, titles, or series
    B. joint authors, series, or subjects
    C. joint authors, titles, or subjects
    D. titles, publishers, or series

18. Which of the following illustrates a directional question?

    A. How far is Syracuse from Lake Ontario?
    B. Where is the public telephone?
    C. Where can I find a biographical dictionary of presidents?
    D. Is Italy to the east of Spain?

19. You are performing an online bibliographic search for a patron and have brought up a set consisting of 300 records.
    Of the following, which is the LEAST valid way of limiting the search in order to avoid printing such a large set?

    A. Limit the search to a certain range of years
    B. Redefine the search using more specific descriptors
    C. Print only the first 40 records of the set
    D. Cut out references to articles in languages the patron cannot read

20. All of the following are examples of primary sources EXCEPT

    A. diaries   B. biographies
    C. letters   D. memoirs

21. *What is the population of Mexico City?* would MOST likely be classified as what type of reference question?

    A. Ready reference   B. Directional
    C. Research on a topic   D. Instructional

22. Something you would NOT expect to find in a vertical file is

    A. a monograph   B. a pamphlet
    C. a folded map   D. newspaper clippings

23. Logical product, logical sum, and logical difference are all part of what type of searching?

    A. Permuterm logic   B. Keyword-in-context (KWIC)
    C. Statistical logic   D. Boolean logic

24. Keyword-in-context (KWIC) indexing is also called _____ indexing.

    A. title   B. comprehensive
    C. subject   D. permutation

46

25. The MARC format was developed at the

   A. National Library of Medicine
   B. British Library
   C. Library of Congress
   D. Smithsonian Institute

26. Patrons of a general library are usually MOST aware of which of the following library activities?

   A. Circulation
   B. Accession
   C. Cataloging
   D. Reference

27. Three of the following four are consequences of the copyrighting of books by the U.S. government.
Which is NOT such a consequence?

   A. Protecting author's rights
   B. Encouraging writing
   C. Securing deposit material for the government
   D. Government endorsement of the copyrighted texts

28. The term *cataloging in publication* refers to a cataloging program under which cataloging information

   A. appears in the PUBLISHERS' WEEKLY
   B. appears in the National Union Catalog
   C. appears in the publication itself
   D. is prepared by the publisher

29. The MAJOR use of a formal statement of a library's objective is

   A. serving as a guideline for program development and services
   B. justifying library staffing to the board and public
   C. convincing the governing body of the need for financial support
   D. training library staff in improved methods and practices

30. Circulation statistics should be gathered PRIMARILY for the purpose of

   A. justifying the library budget
   B. Improving library service
   C. cutting library costs
   D. analyzing personnel performance

KEY (CORRECT ANSWERS)

1. A
2. A
3. C
4. D
5. A

6. B
7. C
8. A
9. A
10. D

11. C
12. C
13. C
14. A
15. D

16. C
17. A
18. B
19. C
20. B

21. A
22. A
23. D
24. D
25. C

26. A
27. D
28. C
29. A
30. B

TEST 3

DIRECTIONS: Each question or incomplete statement is followed by several suggested answers or completions. Select the one that BEST answers the question or completes the statement. *PRINT THE LETTER OF THE CORRECT ANSWER IN THE SPACE AT THE RIGHT.*

1. A typical reference in the READER'S GUIDE TO PERIODICAL LITERATURE would include all of the following EXCEPT

    A. author
    B. title of the article
    C. journal name
    D. journal abstract

    1.____

2. An example of a subject authority list used in cataloging is the

    A. THESAURUS OF ERIC DESCRIPTORS
    B. LIBRARY OF CONGRESS SUBJECT HEADINGS
    C. NEW YORK TIMES INDEX
    D. CINAHL SUBJECT HEADING LIST

    2.____

3. An example of a nonperiodical serial is

    A. EUROPA YEARBOOK
    B. AQUACULTURE MAGAZINE
    C. THE WASHINGTON POST
    D. JOURNAL OF THE AMERICAN MEDICAL ASSOCIATION

    3.____

4. The Superintendent of Documents classification system arranges government documents on the shelves

    A. alphabetically by title
    B. by government agency
    C. alphabetically by author
    D. according to date of printing

    4.____

5. Which of the following is an example of an open-ended question?

    A. Would you like books or magazine articles?
    B. You say you need to know the elevation of Denver?
    C. What kind of information about sharks are you looking for?
    D. Have you ever used our online catalog?

    5.____

6. Scientific Information's weekly CURRENT CONTENTS consists of

    A. reproductions of journal contents pages
    B. a subject index for scientific journals
    C. author and title indexes for current periodicals
    D. scientific journal abstracts

    6.____

7. All of the following are bibliographic utilities involved in resource sharing EXCEPT

    A. OCLC   B. RLIN   C. DYNIX   D. UTLAS

    7.____

49

8. The MAIN objective of reference negotiation is to
    A. save the librarian's time
    B. steer patrons away from heavily used sources
    C. find out what the patron specifically needs
    D. instruct patrons in the proper use of reference materials

9. Which of the following PROPERLY demonstrates a logical product and logical difference search statement?
    A. Dogs and cats, not birds
    B. (Dogs or cats) and not birds
    C. Dogs and not birds or cats
    D. Dogs and (cats or birds)

10. The generally accepted definition of a serial includes all of the following EXCEPT
    A. yearbooks   B. newspapers
    C. theses   D. journals

11. ESSAY AND GENERAL LITERATURE INDEX is MOST useful for locating
    A. a specific chapter of a book
    B. magazine and journal articles
    C. biographical essays
    D. a pamphlet or newsletter

12. What do LIBRARY JOURNAL, SHEEHY'S GUIDE TO REFERENCE BOOKS, and ARBA have in common?
    They
    A. are all periodicals
    B. discuss management of online catalogs
    C. provide critical evaluation of reference materials
    D. discuss only highly recommended reference sources

13. SHORT STORY INDEX covers stories published
    A. on all subjects except science fiction
    B. in collections and the NEW YORK TIMES
    C. in collections and periodicals
    D. by American authors only

14. One way in which nonperiodical serials (such as yearbooks) are different from periodical serials (such as journals) is that nonperiodicals are
    A. published several times a year
    B. usually a collection of articles
    C. usually ordered by subscription
    D. usually acquired through a standing order

15. Of the general serial sources listed below, which is the only one that includes newspapers?　　15.____

    A. STANDARD PERIODICAL DIRECTORY
    B. GALE DIRECTORY OF PUBLICATIONS
    C. ULRICH'S INTERNATIONAL PERIODICALS DIRECTORY
    D. IRREGULAR SERIALS AND ANNUALS

16. The READER'S GUIDE TO PERIODICAL LITERATURE indexes　　16.____

    A. magazines and newspapers
    B. popular magazines
    C. scholarly journals
    D. short story anthologies

17. Ethnic numbers are added to classification symbols so as to arrange books by　　17.____

    A. subject   B. place of printing
    C. author   D. language

18. End-matter items could include all of the following EXCEPT　　18.____

    A. appendices   B. bibliographies
    C. tables of contents   D. indexes

19. Which of the following BEST describes a jobber?　　19.____
    A

    A. company which produces databases
    B. corporate body responsible for placing a book on the market
    C. wholesale bookseller who stocks books and supplies them to libraries
    D. person skilled in writing computer programs

20. The word *an* is a stopword on the Medline database.　　20.____
    This means that

    A. it cannot be used as a search term in the database
    B. Medline includes articles such as *an* and *the* when alphabetizing by title
    C. if you type in that word, you will exit the database
    D. you cannot use Medline when searching for a title that begins with *an*

21. Of the following queries, which could NOT be answered by consulting a regular dictionary?　　21.____

    A. What is the Golden Rule?
    B. How deep is a fathom?
    C. Does "humble" come from the same root as "human"?
    D. What are the rules for writing a sonnet?

22. An accurate definition of annals would be a(n)　　22.____

    A. serial publication issued once a year
    B. anonymous publication
    C. record of events arranged in chronological order
    D. bibliography of an author's writings arranged by date of publication

23. West's FEDERAL PRACTICE DIGEST is an index to   23.____

    A. United States Supreme Court cases
    B. United States statutes
    C. New York State statutes
    D. The Code of Federal Regulations

24. MOST federal government documents are printed by   24.____

    A. the Government Printing Office
    B. the Library of Congress
    C. the United States Printing Office
    D. Congress

25. Setting aside a separate section for oversized books is an example of   25.____

    A. subject cataloging
    B. parallel arrangement
    C. a special materials collection
    D. Dewey Decimal Classification

KEY (CORRECT ANSWERS)

1.	D	11.	A
2.	B	12.	C
3.	A	13.	C
4.	B	14.	D
5.	C	15.	B
6.	A	16.	B
7.	C	17.	D
8.	C	18.	C
9.	A	19.	C
10.	C	20.	A

21. D
22. C
23. A
24. A
25. B

EXAMINATION SECTION
TEST 1

DIRECTIONS: Each question or incomplete statement is followed by several suggested answers or completions. Select the one that BEST answers the question or completes the statement. *PRINT THE LETTER OF THE CORRECT ANSWER IN THE SPACE AT THE RIGHT.*

1. In public agencies, communications should be based PRIMARILY on a 1.____
   A. two-way flow from the top down and from the bottom up, most of which should be given in writing to avoid ambiguity
   B. multi-direction flow among all levels and with outside persons
   C. rapid, internal one-way flow from the top down
   D. two-way flow of information, most of which should be given orally for purposes of clarity

2. In some organizations, changes in policy or procedures are often communicated by word of mouth from supervisors to employees with no prior discussion or exchange of viewpoints with employees. 2.____
   This procedure often produces employee dissatisfaction CHIEFLY because
   A. information is mostly unusable since a considerable amount of time is required to transmit information
   B. lower-level supervisors tend to be excessively concerned with minor details
   C. management has failed to seek employees' advice before making changes
   D. valuable staff time is lost between decision-making and the implementation of decisions

3. For good letter writing, you should try to visualize the person to whom you are writing, especially if you know him. 3.____
   Of the following rules, it is LEAST helpful in such visualization to think of
   A. the person's likes and dislikes, his concerns, and his needs
   B. what you would be likely to say if speaking in person
   C. what you would expect to be asked if speaking in person
   D. your official position in order to be certain that your words are proper

4. One approach to good informal letter writing is to make letters and conversational. 4.____
   All of the following practices will usually help to do this EXCEPT:
   A. If possible, use a style which is similar to the style used when speaking
   B. Substitute phrases for single words (e.g., *at the present time* for *now*)
   C. Use contractions of words (e.g., *you're* for *you are*)
   D. Use ordinary vocabulary when possible

5. All of the following rules will aid in producing clarity in report-writing EXCEPT:
   A. Give specific details or examples, if possible
   B. Keep related words close together in each sentence
   C. Present information in sequential order
   D. Put several thoughts or ideas in each paragraph

6. The one of the following statements about public relations which is MOST accurate is that
   A. in the long run, appearance gains better results than performance
   B. objectivity is decreased if outside public relations consultants are employed
   C. public relations is the responsibility of every employee
   D. public relations should be based on a formal publicity program

7. The form of communication which is usually considered to be MOST personally directed to the intended recipient is the
   A. brochure   B. film   C. letter   D. radio

8. In general, a document that presents an organization's views or opinions on a particular topic is MOST accurately known as a
   A. tear sheet   B. position paper
   C. flyer   D. journal

9. Assume that you have been asked to speak before an organization of persons who oppose a newly announced program in which you are involved. You feel tense about talking to this group.
   Which of the following rules generally would be MOST useful in gaining rapport when speaking before the audience?
   A. Impress them with your experience
   B. Stress all areas of disagreement
   C. Talk to the group as to one person
   D. Use formal grammar and language

10. An organization must have an effective public relations program since, at its best, public relations is a bridge to change.
    All of the following statements about communication and human behavior have validity EXCEPT:
    A. People are more likely to talk about controversial matters with like-minded people than with those holding other views
    B. The earlier an experience, the more powerful its effect since it influences how later experiences will be interpreted
    C. In periods of social tension, official sources gain increased believability
    D. Those who are already interested in a topic are the ones who are most open to receive new communications about it

11. An employee should be encouraged to talk easily and frankly when he is dealing with his supervisor.
    In order to encourage such free communication, it would be MOST appropriate for a supervisor to behave in a(n)
    A. sincere manner; assure the employee that you will deal with him honestly and openly
    B. official manner; you are a supervisor and must always act formally with subordinates
    C. investigative manner; you must probe and question to get to a basis of trust
    D. unemotional manner; the employee's emotions and background should play no part in your dealings with him

11._____

12. Research findings show that an increase in free communication within an agency GENERALLY results in which one of the following?
    A. Improved morale and productivity
    B. Increased promotional opportunities
    C. An increase in authority
    D. A spirit of honesty

12._____

13. Assume that you are a supervisor and your superiors have given you a new-type procedure to be followed.
    Before passing this information on to your subordinates, the one of the following actions that you should take FIRST is to
    A. ask your superiors to send out a memorandum to the entire staff
    B. clarify the procedure in your own mind
    C. set up a training course to provide instruction on the new procedure
    D. write a memorandum to your subordinates

13._____

14. Communication is necessary for an organization to be effective.
    The one of the following which is LEAST important for most communication systems is that
    A. messages are sent quickly and directly to the person who needs them to operate
    B. information should be conveyed understandably and accurately
    C. the method used to transmit information should be kept secret so that security can be maintained
    D. senders of messages must know how their messages are received and acted upon

14._____

15. Which one of the following is the CHIEF advantage of listening willingly to subordinates and encouraging them to talk freely and honestly?
    It
    A. reveals to supervisors the degree to which ideas that are passed down are accepted by subordinates
    B. reduces the participation of subordinates in the operation of the department
    C. encourages subordinates to try for promotion
    D. enables supervisors to learn more readily what the *grapevine* is saying

15._____

16. A supervisor may be informed through either oral or written reports. Which one of the following is an ADVANTAGE of using oral reports?
    A. There is no need for a formal record of the report.
    B. An exact duplicate of the report is not easily transmitted to others.
    C. A good oral report requires little time for preparation.
    D. An oral report involves two-way communication between a subordinate and his supervisor.

17. Of the following, the MOST important reason why supervisors should communicate effectively with the public is to
    A. improve the public's understanding of information that is important for them to know
    B. establish a friendly relationship
    C. obtain information about the kinds of people who come to the agency
    D. convince the public that services are adequate

18. Supervisors should generally NOT use phrases like *too hard*, *too easy*, and *a lot* PRINCIPALLY because such phrases
    A. may be offensive to some minority groups
    B. are too informal
    C. mean different things to different people
    D. are difficult to remember

19. The ability to communicate clearly and concisely is an important element in effective leadership.
    Which of the following statements about oral and written communication is GENERALLY true?
    A. Oral communication is more time-consuming.
    B. Written communication is more likely to be misinterpreted.
    C. Oral communication is useful only in emergencies.
    D. Written communication is useful mainly when giving information to fewer than twenty people.

20. Rumors can often have harmful and disruptive effects on an organization. Which one of the following is the BEST way to prevent rumors from becoming a problem?
    A. Refuse to act on rumors, thereby making them less believable.
    B. Increase the amount of information passed along by the *grapevine*.
    C. Distribute as much factual information as possible.
    D. Provide training in report writing.

21. Suppose that a subordinate asks you about a rumor he has heard. The rumor deals with a subject which your superiors consider *confidential*.
    Which of the following BEST describes how you should answer the subordinate? Tell

A. the subordinate that you don't make the rules and that he should speak to higher ranking officials
B. the subordinate that you will ask your superior for information
C. him only that you cannot comment on the matter
D. him the rumor is not true

22. Supervisors often find it difficult to *get their message across* when instructing newly appointed employees in their various duties.
The MAIN reason for this is generally that the
    A. duties of the employees have increased
    B. supervisor is often so expert in his area that he fails to see it from the learner's point of view
    C. supervisor adapts his instruction to the slowest learner in the group
    D. new employees are younger, less concerned with job security and more interested in fringe benefits

23. Assume that you are discussing a job problem with an employee under your supervision. During the discussion, you see that the man's eyes are turning away from you and that he is not paying attention.
In order to get the man's attention, you should FIRST
    A. ask him to look you in the eye
    B. talk to him about sports
    C. tell him he is being very rude
    D. change your tone of voice

24. As a supervisor, you may find it necessary to conduct meetings with your subordinates.
Of the following, which would be MOST helpful in assuring that a meeting accomplishes the purpose for which it was called?
    A. Give notice of the conclusions you would like to reach at the start of the meeting.
    B. Delay the start of the meeting until everyone is present.
    C. Write down points to be discussed in proper sequence.
    D. Make sure everyone is clear on whatever conclusions have been reached and on what must be done after the meeting.

25. Every supervisor will occasionally be called upon to deliver a reprimand to a subordinate. If done properly, this can greatly help an employee improve his performance.
Which one of the following is NOT a good practice to follow when giving a reprimand?
    A. Maintain your composure and temper
    B. Reprimand a subordinate in the presence of other employees so they can learn the same lesson
    C. Try to understand why the employee was not able to perform satisfactorily
    D. Let your knowledge of the man involved determine the exact nature of the reprimand

KEY (CORRECT ANSWERS)

1. C
2. B
3. D
4. B
5. D

6. C
7. C
8. B
9. C
10. C

11. A
12. A
13. B
14. C
15. A

16. D
17. A
18. C
19. B
20. C

21. B
22. B
23. D
24. D
25. B

TEST 2

DIRECTIONS: Each question or incomplete statement is followed by several suggested answers or completions. Select the one that BEST answers the question or completes the statement. *PRINT THE LETTER OF THE CORRECT ANSWER IN THE SPACE AT THE RIGHT.*

1. Usually one thinks of communication as a single step, essentially that of transmitting an idea.
   Actually, however, this is only part of a total process, the FIRST step of which should be
   A. the prompt dissemination of the idea to those who may be affected by it
   B. motivating those affected to take the required action
   C. clarifying the idea in one's own mind
   D. deciding to whom the idea is to be communicated

   1.____

2. Research studies on patterns of informal communication have concluded that most individuals in a group tend to be passive recipients of news, while a few make it their business to spread it around in an organization.
   With this conclusion in mind, it would be MOST correct for the supervisor to attempt to identify these few individuals and
   A. give them the complete facts on important matters in advance of others
   B. inform the other subordinates of the identity of these few individuals so that their influence may be minimized
   C. keep them straight on the facts on important matters
   D. warn them to cease passing along any information to others

   2.____

3. The one of the following which is the PRINCIPAL advantage of making an oral report is that it
   A. affords an immediate opportunity for two-way communication between the subordinate and superior
   B. is an easy method for the superior to use in transmitting information to others of equal rank
   C. saves the time of all concerned
   D. permits more precise pinpointing of praise or blame by means of follow-up questions by the superior

   3.____

4. An agency may sometimes undertake a public relations program of a defensive nature.
   With reference to the use of defensive public relations, it would be MOST correct to state that it
   A. is bound to be ineffective since defensive statements, even though supported by factual data, can never hope to even partly overcome the effects of prior unfavorable attacks
   B. proves that the agency has failed to establish good relationships with newspapers, radio stations, or other means of publicity

   4.____

C. shows that the upper echelons of the agency have failed to develop sound public relations procedures and techniques
D. is sometimes required to aid morale by protecting the agency from unjustified criticism and misunderstanding of policies or procedures

5. Of the following factors which contribute to possible undesirable public attitudes towards an agency, the one which is MOST susceptible to being changed by the efforts of the individual employee in an organization is that
   A. enforcement of unpopular regulations as offended many individuals
   B. the organization itself has an unsatisfactory reputation
   C. the public is not interested in agency matters
   D. there are many errors in judgment committed by individual subordinates

6. It is not enough for an agency's services to be of a high quality; attention must also be given to the acceptability of these services to the general public.
   This statement is GENERALLY
   A. *false*; a superior quality of service automatically wins public support
   B. *true*; the agency cannot generally progress beyond the understanding and support of the public
   C. *false*; the acceptance by the public of agency services determines their quality
   D. *true*; the agency is generally unable to engage in any effective enforcement activity without public support

7. Sustained agency participation in a program sponsored by a community organization is MOST justified when
   A. the achievement of agency objectives in some area depends partly on the activity of this organization
   B. the community organization is attempting to widen the base of participation in all community affairs
   C. the agency is uncertain as to what the community wants
   D. the agency is uncertain as to what the community wants

8. Of the following, the LEAST likely way in which a records system may serve a supervisor is in
   A. developing a sympathetic and cooperative public attitude toward the agency
   B. improving the quality of supervision by permitting a check on the accomplishment of subordinates
   C. permit a precise prediction of the exact incidences in specific categories for the following year
   D. helping to take the guesswork out of the distribution of the agency

9. Assuming that the *grapevine* in any organization is virtually indestructible, the one of the following which it is MOST important for management to understand is:
   A. What is being spread by means of the *grapevine* and the reason for spreading it
   B. What is being spread by means of the *grapevine* and how it is being spread
   C. Who is involved in spreading the information that is on the *grapevine*
   D. Why those who are involved in spreading the information are doing so

9.____

10. When the supervisor writes a report concerning an investigation to which he has been assigned, it should be LEAST intended to provide
    A. a permanent official record of relevant information gathered
    B. a summary of case findings limited to facts which tend to indicate the guilt of a suspect
    C. a statement of the facts on which higher authorities may base a corrective or disciplinary action
    D. other investigators with information so that they may continue with other phases of the investigation

10.____

11. In survey work, questionnaires rather than interviews are sometimes used. The one of the following which is a DISADVANTAGE of the questionnaire method as compared with the interview is the
    A. difficulty of accurately interpreting the results
    B. problem of maintaining anonymity of the participant
    C. fact that it is relatively uneconomical
    D. requirement of special training for the distribution of questionnaires

11.____

12. In his contacts with the public, an employee should attempt to create a good climate of support for his agency.
    This statement is GENERALLY
    A. *false*; such attempts are clearly beyond the scope of his responsibility
    B. *true*; employees of an agency who come in contact with the public have the opportunity to affect public relations
    C. *false*; such activity should be restricted to supervisors trained in public relations techniques
    D. *true*; the future expansion of the agency depends to a great extent on continued public support of the agency

12.____

13. The repeated use by a supervisor of a call for volunteers to get a job done is objectionable MAINLY because it
    A. may create a feeling of animosity between the volunteers and the non-volunteers
    B. may indicate that the supervisor is avoiding responsibility for making assignments which will be most productive
    C. is an indication that the supervisor is not familiar with the individual capabilities of his men
    D. is unfair to men who, for valid reasons, do not, or cannot volunteer

13.____

14. Of the following statements concerning subordinates' expressions to a supervisor of their opinions and feelings concerning work situations, the one which is MOST correct is that
    A. by listening and responding to such expressions the supervisor encourages the development of complaints
    B. the lack of such expressions should indicate to the supervisor that there is a high level of job satisfaction
    C. the more the supervisor listens to and responds to such expressions, the more he demonstrates lack of supervisory ability
    D. by listening and responding to such expressions, the supervisor will enable many subordinates to understand and solve their own problems on the job

15. In attempting to motivate employees, rewards are considered preferable to punishment PRIMARILY because
    A. punishment seldom has any effect on human behavior
    B. punishment usually results in decreased production
    C. supervisors find it difficult to punish
    D. rewards are more likely to result in willing cooperation

16. In an attempt to combat the low morale in his organization, a high level supervisor publicized an *open-door policy* to allow employees who wished to do so to come to him with their complaints.
    Which of the following is LEAST likely to account for the fact that no employee came in with a complaint?
    A. Employees are generally reluctant to go over the heads of their immediate supervisor.
    B. The employees did not feel that management would help them.
    C. The low morale was not due to complaints associated with the job.
    D. The employees felt that they had more to lose than to gain.

17. It is MOST desirable to use written instructions rather than oral instructions for a particular job when
    A. a mistake on the job will not be serious
    B. the job can be completed in a short time
    C. there is no need to explain the job minutely
    D. the job involves many details

18. If you receive a telephone call regarding a matter which your office does not handle, you should FIRST
    A. give the caller the telephone number of the proper office so that he can dial again
    B. offer to transfer the caller to the proper office
    C. suggest that the caller re-dial since he probably dialed incorrectly
    D. tell the caller he has reached the wrong office and then hang up

19. When you answer the telephone, the MOST important reason for identifying yourself and your organization is to
    A. give the caller time to collect his or her thoughts
    B. impress the caller with your courtesy
    C. inform the caller that he or she has reached the right number
    D. set a business-like tone at the beginning of the conversation

    19.____

20. As soon as you pick up the phone, a very angry caller begins immediately to complain about city agencies and *red tape*. He says that he has been shifted to two or three different offices. It turs out that he is seeking information which is not immediately available to you. You believe, you know, however, where it can be found.
    Which of the following actions is the BEST one for you to take?
    A. To eliminate all confusion, suggest that the caller write the agency stating explicitly what he wants.
    B. Apologize by telling the caller how busy city agencies now are, but also tell him directly that you do not have the information he needs.
    C. Ask for the caller's telephone number and assure him you will call back after you have checked further.
    D. Give the caller the name and telephone number of the person who might be able to help, but explain that you are not positive he will get results/

    20.____

21. Which of the following approaches usually provides the BEST communication in the objectives and values of a new program which is to be introduced?
    A. A general written description of the program by the program manager for review by those who share responsibility
    B. An effective verbal presentation by the program manager to those affected
    C. Development of the plan and operational approach in carrying out the program by the program manager assisted by his key subordinates
    D. Development of the plan by the program manager's supervisor

    21.____

22. What is the BEST approach for introducing change?
    A
    A. combination of written and also verbal communication to all personnel affected by the change
    B. general bulletin to all personnel
    C. meeting pointing out all the values of the new approach
    D. written directive to key personnel

    22.____

23. Of the following, committees are BEST used for
    A. advising the head of the organization
    B. improving functional work
    C. making executive decisions
    D. making specific planning decisions

    23.____

24. An effective discussion leader is one who
    A. announces the problem and his preconceived solution at the start of the discussion
    B. guides and directs the discussion according to pre-arranged outline
    C. interrupts or corrects confused participants to save time
    D. permits anyone to say anything at any time

25. The human relations movement in management theory is basically concerned with
    A. counteracting employee unrest
    B. eliminating the *time and motion* man
    C. interrelationships among individuals in organizations
    D. the psychology of the worker

KEY (CORRECT ANSWERS)

1.	C	11.	A
2.	C	12.	B
3.	A	13.	B
4.	D	14.	D
5.	D	15.	D
6.	B	16.	C
7.	A	17.	D
8.	C	18.	B
9.	A	19.	C
10.	B	20.	C

21.	C
22.	A
23.	A
24.	B
25.	C

SUPERVISION, ADMINISTRATION, MANAGEMENT, AND ORGANIZATION

EXAMINATION SECTION

TEST 1

DIRECTIONS: Each question or incomplete statement is followed by several suggested answers or completions. Select the one that BEST answers the question or completes the statement. *PRINT THE LETTER OF THE CORRECT ANSWER IN THE SPACE AT THE RIGHT.*

1. A supervisor scheduled and interview with a subordinate in order to discuss his unsatisfactory performance during the previous several weeks. The subordinate's work contained an excessive number of careless errors.
After the interview, the supervisor, reviewing his own approach for self-examination, listed three techniques he had used in the interview, as follows:
   I. Specifically pointed out to the subordinate where he had failed to meet the standards expected.
   II. Shared the blame for certain management errors that had irritated the subordinate.
   III. Agreed with the subordinate on specific targets to be met during the period ahead.
   Of the following statements, the one that is MOST acceptable concerning the above three techniques is that
      A. all 3 techniques are correct
      B. techniques I and II are correct; III is not correct
      C. techniques II and III are correct; I is not correct
      D. techniques I and III are correct; II is not correct

2. Assume that the performance of an employee is not satisfactory.
Of the following, the MOST effective way for a supervisor to attempt to improve the performance of the employee is to meet with him and to
      A. order him to change his behavior
      B. indicate the actions that are unsatisfactory and the penalties for them
      C. show him alternate ways of behaving and a method for him to evaluate his attempts at change
      D. suggest that he use the behavior of the supervisor as a model of acceptable conduct

3. Training employees to be productive workers is based on four fundamental principles:
   I. Demonstrate how the job should be done by telling and showing the correct operations step-by-step
   II. Allow the employee to get some of the feel of the job by allowing him to try it a bit
   III. Put him on the job while continuing to check his performance
   IV. Let him know why the job is important and why it must be done right

1.____

2.____

3.____

65

The MOST logical order for these training steps is:
A. I, III, II, IV   B. I, IV, II, III   C. II, I, III, IV   D. IV, I, II, III

4. Sometimes a supervisor is faced with the need to train under-educated new employees.
   The following five statements relate to training such employees.
   I. Make the training general rather than specific
   II. Rely upon demonstrations and illustrations whenever possible
   III. Overtrain rather than undertrain by erring on the side of imparting a little more skill than is absolutely necessary
   IV. Provide lots of follow-up on the job
   V. Reassure and recognize frequently in order to increase self-confidence
   Which of the following choices lists all the above statements that are generally CORRECT?
   A. I, II, IV   B. II, III, IV, V   C. I, II, V   D. I, II, IV, V

5. One of the ways in which some supervisors train subordinates is to discuss the subordinate's weaknesses with them. Experts who have explored the actual feelings and reactions of subordinates in such situations have come to the conclusion that such interviews USUALLY
   A. are seen by subordinates as a threat to their self-esteem
   B. give subordinates a feeling of importance which leads to better learning
   C. convince subordinates to accept the opinion of the supervisor
   D. result in the development of better supervision

6. The one of the following which BEST describes the rate at which a trainee learns departmental procedures is that he *probably* will learn
   A. at the same rate throughout if the material to be learned is complex
   B. slowly in the beginning and then learning will accelerate steadily
   C. quickly for a while, than slow down temporarily
   D. at the same rate if the material to be learned is lengthy

7. Which of the following statements concerning the delegation of work to subordinate employees is generally CORRECT?
   A. A supervisor's personal attitude toward delegation has a minimal effect on his skill in delegating.
   B. A willingness to let subordinates make mistakes has a place in work delegation.
   C. The element of trust has little impact on the effectiveness of work delegation.
   D. The establishment of controls does not enhance the process of delegation.

8. Assume that you are the chairman of a group that has been formed to discuss and solve a particular problem. After a half-hour of discussion, you feel that the group is wandering off the point and is no longer discussing the problem.
   In this situation, it would be BEST for you to
   A. wait to see whether the group will get back on the track by itself
   B. ask the group to stop and to try a different approach

C. ask the group to stop, decide where they are going, and then to decide how to continue
D. ask the group to stop, decide where they are going, and then to continue in a different direction

9. One method of group decision-making is the use of committees. Following are four statements concerning committees.
   I. Considering the value of each individual member's time, committees are costly.
   II. One result of committee decisions is that no one may be held responsible for the decision.
   III. Committees will make decisions more promptly than individuals.
   IV. Committee decisions tend to be balanced and to take different viewpoints into account.
   Which of the following choices lists all of the above statements that are generally CORRECT?
   A. I and II   B. II and III   C. I, II, IV   D. II, III, IV

10. Assume that an employee bypasses his supervisor and comes directly to you, the superior officer, to ask for a short leave of absence because of a pressing personal problem. The employee did not first consult with his immediate supervisor because he believes that his supervisor is unfavorably biased against him.
    Of the following, the MOST desirable way for you to handle this situation is to
    A. instruct the employee that is it not appropriate for him to go over the head of his supervisor regardless of their personal relationship
    B. listen to a brief description of his problem and then tactfully suggest that he take the matter up with his supervisor before coming to you
    C. request that both the employee and his supervisor meet jointly with you in order to discuss the employee's problem and to get at the reasons behind their apparent difficulty
    D. listen carefully to the employee's problem and then, without committing yourself one way or the other, promise to discuss it with his supervisor

11. Which of the following statements concerning the motivation of subordinates is generally INCORRECT? The
    A. authoritarian approach as the method of supervision is likely to result in the setting of minimal performance standards for themselves by subordinates
    B. encouragement of competition among subordinates may lead to deterioration of teamwork
    C. granting of benefits by a supervisor to subordinates in order to gain their gratitude will result in maximum output by the subordinates
    D. opportunity to achieve job satisfaction has an important effect on motivating subordinates

12. Of the following, the MOST serious disadvantage of having a supervisor evaluate subordinates on the basis of measurable performance goals that are set jointly by the supervisor and the subordinates is that this results-oriented appraisal method
    A. focuses on past performance rather than plans for the future
    B. fails to provide sufficient feedback to help subordinates learn where they stand
    C. encourages the subordinates to conceal poor performance and set low goals
    D. changes the primary task of the supervisor from helping subordinates improve to criticizing their performance

13. A supervisor can BEST provide on-the-job satisfaction for his subordinates by
    A. providing rewards for good performance
    B. allowing them to decide when to do the assigned work
    C. motivating them to perform according to accepted procedures
    D. providing challenging work that achieves departmental objectives

14. Which of the following factors generally contributes MOST to job satisfaction among supervisory employees?
    A. Autonomy and independence on the job
    B. Job security
    C. Pleasant physical working conditions
    D. Adequate economic rewards

15. Large bureaucracies typically exhibit certain characteristics.
    Of the following, it would be CORRECT to state that such bureaucracies generally
    A. tend to oversimplify communications
    B. pay undue attention to informal organizations
    C. develop an attitude of "group-think" and conformity
    D. emphasize personal growth among employees

16. When positive methods fail to achieve conformity with accepted standards of conduct or performance, a negative type of action, punitive in nature, usually must follow.
    The one of the following that is usually considered LEAST important for the success of such punishment or negative discipline is that it be
    A. certain   B. swift   C. severe   D. consistent

17. Assume that you are a supervisor. Philip Smith, who is under your supervision, informs you that James Jones, who is also your subordinate, has been creating antagonism and friction within the unit because of his unnecessarily gruff manner in dealing with his co-workers. Smith's remarks confirm your own observations of Jones' behavior and its effects.

In handling this situation, the one of the following procedures which will probably be MOST effective is to
A. ask Smith to act as an informal counselor to Jones and report the results to you
B. counsel the other employees in your unit on methods of changing attitudes of people
C. interview Jones and help him to understand this problem
D. order Jones to carry out his responsibilities with greater consideration for the feelings of his co-workers

18. The principle relating to the number of subordinates who can be supervised effectively by one supervisor is COMMONLY known as
    A. span of control   B. delegation of authority
    C. optimum personnel assignment   D. organizational factor

18.____

19. Ascertaining and improving the level of morale in a public agency is one of the responsibilities of a conscientious supervisor.
    The one of the following aspects of subordinates' behavior which is NOT an indication of low morale is
    A. lower-level employees participating in organizational decision-making
    B. careless treatment of equipment
    C. general deterioration of personal appearance
    D. formation of cliques

19.____

20. Employees may resist changes in agency operations even though such changes are often necessary. If you, as a supervisor, are attempting to introduce a necessary change, you should first fully explain the reasons for it to your staff.
    Your NEXT step should be to
    A. set specific goals and outline programs for all employees
    B. invite employee participation in effectuating the change by asking for suggestions to accomplish it
    C. discuss the need for improved work performance by city employees
    D. point out the penalties for non-cooperation without singling out any employee by name

20.____

21. A supervisor should normally void giving orders in an offhand or casual manner MAINLY because his subordinates
    A. are like most people and may resent being treated lightly
    B. may attach little importance to these orders
    C. may work best if given the choice of work methods
    D. are unlikely to need instructions in most matters

21.____

22. Assume that, as a supervisor, you have just praised a subordinate. While he expresses satisfaction at your praise, he complains that it does not help him get promoted even though he is on a promotion eligible list, since there is no current vacancy.

22.____

In these circumstances, it would be BEST for you to
- A. minimize the importance of advancement and emphasize the satisfaction in the work itself
- B. follow up by pointing out some errors he has committed in the past
- C. admit that the situation exists, and express the hope that it will improve
- D. tell him that, until quite recently, advancement was even slower

23. Departmental policies are usually broad rules or guides for action. It is important for a supervisor to understand his role with respect to policy implementation.
    Of the following, the MOST accurate description of this role is that a supervisor should
    - A. be apologetic toward his subordinates when applying unpopular policies to them
    - B. act within policy limits, although he can attempt to influence policy change by making his thoughts and observations known to his superior
    - C. arrange his activities so that he is able to deal simultaneously with situations that involve several policy matters
    - D. refrain as much as possible from exercising permissible discretion in applying policy to matters under his control

24. A supervisor should be aware that most subordinates will ask questions at meetings or group discussions in order to
    - A. stimulate other employees to express their opinions
    - B. discover how they may be affected by the subjects under discussion
    - C. display their knowledge of the topics under discussion
    - D. consume time in order to avoid returning to their normal tasks

25. Don't assign responsibilities with conflicting objectives to the same work group. For example, to require a unit to monitor the quality of its own work is a bad practice.
    This practice is MOST likely to be bad because
    - A. the chain of command will be unnecessarily lengthened
    - B. it is difficult to portray mixed duties accurately on an organization chart
    - C. employees may act in collusion to cover up poor work
    - D. the supervisor may delegate responsibilities which he should retain

KEY (CORRECT ANSWERS)

1.	A	11.	C
2.	C	12.	C
3.	D	13.	D
4.	B	14.	A
5.	A	15.	C
6.	C	16.	C
7.	B	17.	C
8.	C	18.	A
9.	C	19.	A
10.	D	20.	B

21. B
22. C
23. B
24. B
25. C

TEST 2

DIRECTIONS: Each question or incomplete statement is followed by several suggested answers or completions. Select the one that BEST answers the question or completes the statement. *PRINT THE LETTER OF THE CORRECT ANSWER IN THE SPACE AT THE RIGHT.*

1. Some supervisors use an approach in which each phase of the job is explained in broad terms supervision is general, and employees are allowed broad discretion in performing their job duties.
Such a supervisory approach USUALLY affects employee motivation by
   A. improving morale and providing an incentive to work harder
   B. providing little or no incentive to work harder than the minimum required
   C. creating extra pressure, usually resulting in decreased performance
   D. reducing incentive to work and causing employees to feel neglected, particularly in performing complex tasks

1.____

2. An employee complains to a superior officer that he has been treated unfairly by his supervisor, stating that other employees have been given less work to do and shown other forms of favoritism.
Of the following, the BEST thing for the superior officer to do FIRST in order to handle this problem is to
   A. try to discover whether the subordinate has a valid complaint or if something else is the real problem
   B. ask other employees whether they feel their treatment is consistent and fair
   C. ask his supervisor to explain the charges
   D. see that the number of cases assigned to this employee is reduced

2.____

3. Of the following, the MOST important condition needed to help a group of people to work well together and get the job done is
   A. higher salaries and a better working environment
   B. enough free time to relieve the tension
   C. good communication among everyone involved in the job
   D. assurance that everyone likes the work

3.____

4. A supervisor realizes that a subordinate has called in sick for three Mondays out of the past four. These absences have interfered with staff performance and have been part of the cause of the unit's "behind schedule" condition.
In order to correct this situation, it would be BEST for the supervisor to
   A. order the subordinate to explain his abuse of sick leave
   B. discuss with the subordinate the penalties for abusing sick leave
   C. discuss the matter with his own supervisor
   D. ask the subordinate in private whether he has a problem about coming to work

4.____

5. Of the following, the MOST effective way for a supervisor to minimize undesirable rumors about new policies in the units under his supervision is to
   A. bypass the supervisor and communicate directly with the individual members of the units
   B. supply immediate and accurate information to everyone who is supposed to be informed
   C. play down the importance of the rumors
   D. issue all communications in written form

6. Which of the following is an indication that a superior officer is delegating authority PROPERLY?
   A. The superior officer closely checks the work of experienced subordinates at all stages in order to maintain standards.
   B. The superior officer gives overlapping assignments to insure that work is completed on time.
   C. The work of his subordinates can proceed and be completed during the superior officer's absence.
   D. The work of each supervisor is reviewed by him more than once in order to insure quality.

7. Of the following supervisory practices, the one which is MOST likely to foster employee morale is for the supervisor to
   A. take an active interest in subordinates' personal lives
   B. ignore mistakes
   C. give praise when justified
   D. permit rules to go unenforced occasionally

8. As the supervisor who is responsible for the implementation of new paperwork procedure, you note that the workers often do not follow the stipulated procedure.
   Before taking action, it would be ADVISABLE to realize that
   A. unconscious behavior, such as failure to adapt to change, is largely uncontrollable
   B. new procedures sometimes have to be modified and adapted after being tried out
   C. threats of disciplinary action will encourage approval of change
   D. procedures that fail should be abandoned and replaced

9. The one of the following which is generally considered to be the MOST significant criticism of the modern practice of effective human relations in management of large organizations is that human relations
   A. weakens management authority over employees
   B. gives employees control of operations
   C. can be used to manipulate and control employees
   D. weakens unions

10. Of the following, the MOST important reason why the supervisor should promote good supervisor-subordinate relations is to encourage his staff to
    A. feel important
    B. be more receptive to control
    C. be happy in their work
    D. meet production performance levels

11. A superior officer decides to assign a special report directly to an employee, bypassing his supervisor.
    In general, this practice is
    A. *advisable*, chiefly because it broadens the superior officer's span of authority
    B. *inadvisable*, chiefly because it undermines the authority of the supervisor in the eyes of his subordinates
    C. *advisable*, chiefly because it reduces the number of details the supervisor must know
    D. *inadvisable*, chiefly because it gives too much work to the employee

12. Many supervisors make it a practice to solicit suggestions from their subordinates and to encourage their participation in decision-making.
    The success of this type of supervision usually depends MOST directly upon the
    A. quality of leadership provided by the supervisor
    B. number of the supervisor's immediate subordinates
    C. availability of opportunities for employee advancement
    D. degree to which work assignments cause problems

13. Small informal groups or "cliques" often appear in a work setting.
    The one of the following which is generally an advantage of such groups, from an administrative point of view, is that they
    A. are not influenced by the administrative set-up of the office
    B. encourage socializing after working hours
    C. develop leadership roles among the office staff
    D. provide a "steam valve" for release of tension and fatigue

14. Assume that you are a superior officer in charge of several supervisors who, in turn, are in charge of a number of employees. The employees who are supervised by Jones (a supervisor) come as a group to you and indicate several reasons why Jones is incompetent and "has to go."
    Of the following, your BEST course of action to take FIRST is to
    A. direct the employees to see Jones about the matter
    B. suggest to the employees that they should attempt to work with Jones until he can be transferred
    C. discuss the possibility of terminating Jones with your superior
    D. ask Jones about the comments of the employees after they depart

15. Of the following, the MAIN effect which the delegation of authority can have on the efficiency of an organization is to
    A. reduce the risk of decision-making errors
    B. produce uniformity of policy and action
    C. facilitate speedier decisions and actions
    D. enable closer control of operations

    15.____

16. Of the following, the main DISADVANTAGE of temporarily transferring a newly appointed worker to another unit because of an unexpected vacancy is that the temporary nature of his assignment will, MOST likely,
    A. undermine his incentive to orient himself to his new job
    B. interfere with his opportunities for future advancement
    C. result in friction between himself and his new co-workers
    D. place his new supervisor in a difficult and awkward position

    16.____

17. Assume that you, as a supervisor, have decided to raise the quality of work produced by your subordinates.
    The BEST of the following procedures for you to follow is to
    A. develop mathematically precise standards
    B. appoint a committee of subordinates to set firm and exacting guidelines, including penalties for deviations
    C. modify standards developed by supervisors in other organizations
    D. provide consistent evaluation of subordinates' work, furnishing training whenever advisable

    17.____

18. Assume that a supervisor under your supervision strongly objects whenever changes are proposed which would improve the efficiency of his unit.
    Of the following, the MOST desirable way for you to change his attitude is to
    A. involve him in the planning and formulation of changes
    B. promise to recommend him for a more challenging assignment if he accepts changes
    C. threaten to have him transferred to another unit if he does not accept changes
    D. ask him to go along with the changes on a tentative, trial basis

    18.____

19. Work goals may be defined in terms of units produced or in terms of standards of performance.
    Which of the following statements concerning work goals is CORRECT?
    A. Workers who have a share in establishing goals tend to set a fairly high standard for themselves, but fail to work toward it.
    B. Workers tend to produce according to what they believe are the goals actually expected of them.
    C. Since workers usually produce less than the established goals, management should set goals higher than necessary.
    D. The individual differences of workers can be minimized by using strict goals and invariable procedures.

    19.____

20. Of the following, the type of employee who would respond BEST to verbal instructions given in the form of a suggestion or wish is the
    A. experienced worker who is eager to please
    B. sensitive and emotional worker
    C. hostile worker who is somewhat lazy
    D. slow and methodical worker

21. As a supervisor, you note that the output of an experienced staff member has dropped dramatically during the last two months. In addition, his error rate is significantly above that of other staff members. When you ask the employee the reason for his poor performance, he says, "Well, it's rather personal and I would rather not talk about it if you don't mind."
    At this point, which of the following would be the BEST reply?
    A. Tell him that you will give him two weeks to improve or you will discuss the matter with your own supervisor
    B. Insist that he tell you the reason for his poor work and assure him that anything personal will be kept confidential
    C. Say that you don't want to interfere, but, at the same time, his work has deteriorated, and that you're concerned about it
    D. Explain in a friendly manner that you are going to place a warning letter in his personnel folder that states he has one month in which to improve

22. Research studies have shown that employees who are strongly interested in achievement and advancement on the job usually want assignments where the chance of success is _____, and desire _____ supervisory evaluation of their performance.
    A. low; frequent
    B. high; general
    C. high; infrequent
    D. moderate; specific

23. Of the following, a function of the supervisor that concerns itself with the process of determining a course of action from alternatives is USUALLY referred to as
    A. decentralization
    B. planning
    C. controlling
    D. input

24. Favorable working conditions are an important variable in producing an effective work unit.
    Which of the following would be LEAST conducive in providing a favorable work situation?
    A. Applying a job enrichment program to a routine clerical position
    B. Setting practical goals for the work unit which are consistent with the overall objective of the agency
    C. Assigning individuals to positions which require a higher level of educational achievement than that which they possess
    D. Establishing a communications system which distributes information and provides feedback to all organizational levels

25. Ever supervisor within an organization should know to whom he reports and who reports to him.
Within the organization, this will MOST likely insure
   A. unity of command
   B. confidentiality of sensitive issues
   C. excellent morale
   D. the elimination of the grapevine

KEY (CORRECT ANSWERS)

1.	A	11.	B
2.	A	12.	A
3.	C	13.	D
4.	D	14.	D
5.	B	15.	C
6.	C	16.	A
7.	C	17.	D
8.	B	18.	A
9.	C	19.	B
10.	D	20.	A

21. C
22. D
23. B
24. C
25. A

TEST 3

DIRECTIONS: Each question or incomplete statement is followed by several suggested answers or completions. Select the one that BEST answers the question or completes the statement. *PRINT THE LETTER OF THE CORRECT ANSWER IN THE SPACE AT THE RIGHT.*

1. In trying to improve the motivation of his subordinates, a supervisor can achieve the BEST results by taking action based upon the assumption that *most* employees 1.____
   A. have an inherent dislike of work
   B. wish to be closely directed
   C. are more interested in security than in assuming responsibility
   D. will exercise self-direction without coercion

2. Supervisors in public departments have many functions. 2.____
   Of the following, the function which is LEAST appropriate for a supervisor is to
   A. serve as a deputy for the administrator within his own unit
   B. determine needs within his unit and plan programs to meet these needs
   C. supervise, train, and evaluate all personnel assigned to his unit
   D. initiate and carry out fundraising projects, such as bazaars and carnivals, to buy needed equipment

3. When there are conflicts or tensions between top management and lower-level employees in any public department, the supervisor should FIRSTS attempt to 3.____
   A. represent and enforce the management point of view
   B. act as the representative of the workers to get their ideas across to management
   C. serve as a two-way spokesman, trying to interpret each side to the other
   D. remain neutral, but keep informed of changes in the situation

4. A probationary period for new employees is usually provided in public agencies. 4.____
   The MAJOR purpose of such a period is usually to
   A. allow a determination of employee's suitability for the position
   B. obtain evidence as to employee's ability to perform in a higher position
   C. conform to requirement that ethnic hiring goals be met for all positions
   D. train the new employee in the duties of the position

5. An effective program of orientation for new employees usually includes all of the following EXCEPT 5.____
   A. having the supervisor introduce the new employee to his job, outlining his responsibilities and how to carry them out
   B. permitting the new worker to tour the facility or department, so he can observe all parts of it in action
   C. scheduling meetings for new employees, at which the job requirements are explained to them and they are given personnel manuals
   D. testing the new worker on his skills, and sending him to a centralized in-service workshop

6. In-service training is an important responsibility of supervisors. The MAJOR reason for such training is to
   A. avoid future grievance procedures, because employees might say they were not prepared to carry out their jobs
   B. maximize the effectiveness of the department by helping each employee perform at his full potential
   C. satisfy inspection teams from central headquarters of the department
   D. help prevent disagreements with members of the community

7. There are many forms of useful in-service training. Of the following, the training method which is NOT an appropriate technique for leadership development is to
   A. provide special workshops or clinics in activity skills
   B. conduct pre-season institutes to familiarize new workers with the program of the department and with their roles
   C. schedule team meetings for problem-solving, including both supervisors and leaders
   D. have the leader rate himself on an evaluation form periodically

8. Of the following techniques of evaluating work training programs, the one that is BEST is to
   A. pass out a carefully designed questionnaire to the trainees at the completion of the program
   B. test the knowledge that trainees have both at the beginning of training and at its completion
   C. interview the trainees at the completion of the program
   D. evaluate performance before and after training for both a control group and an experimental group

9. Assume that a new supervisor is having difficulty making his instructions to subordinates clearly understood. The one of the following which is the FIRST step he should take in dealing with this problem is to
   A. set up a training workshop in communication skills
   B. determine the extent and nature of the communication gap
   C. repeat both verbal and written instructions several times
   D. simplify his written and spoken vocabulary

10. Discipline of employees is usually a supervisor's responsibility. There may be several useful forms of disciplinary action in public employment. Of the following, the form that is LEAST appropriate is the
    A. written reprimand or warning
    B. involuntary transfer to another work setting
    C. demotion or suspension
    D. assignment of added hours of work each week

11. Of the following, the MOST effective means of dealing with employee disciplinary problems is to
    A. give personality tests to individuals to identify their psychological problems
    B. distribute and discuss a policy manual containing exact rules governing employee behavior
    C. establish a single, clear penalty to be imposed for all wrongdoing irrespective of degree
    D. have supervisors get to know employees well through social mingling

11.____

12. A recently developed technique for appraising work performance is to have the supervisor record on a continual basis all significant incidents in each subordinate's behavior that indicate unsuccessful action and those that indicate poor behavior.
    Of the following, a major DISADVANTAGE of this method of performance appraisal is that it
    A. often leads to overly close supervision
    B. results in competition among those subordinates being evaluated
    C. tends to result in superficial judgments
    D. lacks objectivity for evaluating performance

12.____

13. Assume that you are a supervisor and have observed the performance of an employee during a period of time. You have concluded that his performance needs improvement.
    In order to approve his performance, it would, therefore, be BEST for you to
    A. note your findings in the employee's personnel folder so that his behavior is a matter of record
    B. report the findings to the personnel officer so he can take prompt action
    C. schedule a problem-solving conference with the employee
    D. recommend his transfer to simpler duties

13.____

14. When an employee's absences or latenesses seem to be nearing excessiveness, the supervisor should speak with him to find out what the problem is.
    Of the following, if such a discussion produces no reasonable explanation, the discussion usually BEST serves to
    A. affirm clearly the supervisor's adherence to proper policy
    B. alert other employees that such behavior is unacceptable
    C. demonstrate that the supervisor truly represents higher management
    D. notify the employee that his behavior is being observed and evaluated

14.____

15. Assume that an employee willfully and recklessly violates an important agency regulation. The nature of the violation is of such magnitude that it demands immediate action, but the facts of the case are not entirely clear. Further assume that the supervisor is free to make any of the following recommendations.

15.____

The MOST appropriate action for the supervisor to take is to recommend that the employee be
A. discharged   B. suspended   C. forced to resign   D. transferred

16. Although employees' titles may be identical, each position in that title may be considerably different.
Of the following, a supervisor should carefully assign each employee to a specific position based PRIMARILY on the employee's
A. capability   B. experience   C. education   D. seniority

17. The one of the following situations where it is MOST appropriate to transfer an employee to a *similar* assignment is one in which the employee
A. lacks motivation and interest
B. experiences a personality conflict with his supervisor
C. is negligent in the performance of his duties
D. lacks capacity or ability to perform assigned tasks

18. The one of the following which is LEAST likely to be affected by improvement in the morale of personnel is employee
A. skill   B. absenteeism   C. turnover   D. job satisfaction

19. The one of the following situations in which it is LEAST appropriate for a supervisor to delegate authority to subordinates is where the supervisor
A. lacks confidence in his own abilities to perform certain work
B. is overburdened and cannot handle all his responsibilities
C. refers all disciplinary problems to his subordinate
D. has to deal with an emergency or crisis

20. Of the following, the BEST attitude toward the use of volunteers in programs is that volunteers should be
A. discouraged, since they cannot be depended upon to show up regularly
B. employed as a last resort when paid personnel are unavailable
C. seen as an appropriate means of providing leadership, when effectively recruited and supervised
D. eliminated to raise the professionalism of personnel

21. A supervisor finds that he is spending too much time on routine tasks, and not enough time on coordinating the work of his employees.
It would be MOST advisable for this supervisor to
A. delegate the task of work coordination to a capable subordinate
B. eliminate some of the routine tasks that the unit is required to perform
C. assign some of the routine tasks to his subordinates
D. postpone the performance of routine tasks until he has achieved proper coordination of his employees' work

22. Of the following, the MOST important reason for having an office manual in looseleaf form rather than in permanent binding is that the looseleaf form
    A. facilitates the addition of new material and the removal of obsolete material
    B. permits several people to use different sections of the manual at the same time
    C. is less expensive to prepare than permanent binding
    D. is more durable than permanent binding

23. In his first discussion with a newly appointed employee, the LEAST important of the following topics for a supervisor of a unit to include is the
    A. duties the subordinate is expected to perform on the job
    B. functions of the unit
    C. methods of determining standards of performance
    D. nature and duration of the training the subordinate will receive on the job

24. A supervisor has just been told by a subordinate, Mr. Jones, that another employee, Mr. Smith, deliberately disobeyed an important rule of the department by taking home some confidential departmental material.
    Of the following courses of action, it would be MOST advisable for the supervisor FIRST to
    A. discuss the matter privately, with both Mr. Jones and Mr. Smith at the same time
    B. call a meeting of the entire staff and discuss the matter generally without mentioning any employee by name
    C. arrange to supervise Mr. Smith's activities more closely
    D. discuss the matter privately with Mr. Smith

25. The one of the following actions which would be MOST efficient and economical for a supervisor to take to minimize the effect of seasonal fluctuations in the workload of his unit is to
    A. increase his permanent staff until it is large enough to handle the work of the busy season
    B. request the purchase of time and labor-saving equipment to be used primarily during the busy season
    C. lower, temporarily, the standards for quality of work performance during peak loads
    D. schedule for the slow season work that it is not essential to perform during the busy season

KEY (CORRECT ANSWERS)

1.	D		11.	B
2.	D		12.	A
3.	C		13.	C
4.	A		14.	D
5.	D		15.	B
6.	B		16.	A
7.	D		17.	B
8.	D		18.	A
9.	B		19.	C
10.	D		20.	C

21. C
22. A
23. C
24. D
25. D

TEST 4

DIRECTIONS: Each question or incomplete statement is followed by several suggested answers or completions. Select the one that BEST answers the question or completes the statement. *PRINT THE LETTER OF THE CORRECT ANSWER IN THE SPACE AT THE RIGHT.*

1. Assume that, while instructing a worker on a new procedure, the instructor asks, at frequent intervals, whether there are any questions.
   His asking for questions is a
   A. *good practice*, because it affords the worker an opportunity to participate actively in the lesson
   B. *good practice*, because it may reveal points that are not understood by the worker
   C. *poor practice*, because workers generally find it embarrassing to ask questions
   D. *poor practice*, because it may result in wasting time on irrelevant matters

2. Any person thoroughly familiar with the specific steps in a particular type of work is well-qualified to serve as a training course instructor in the work.
   This statement is *erroneous* CHIEFLY because
   A. a qualified instructor cannot be expected to have detailed information about many specific fields
   B. a person who knows a field thoroughly may not be good at passing his knowledge along to others
   C. it is practically impossible for any instructor to be acquainted with all the specific steps in a particular type of work
   D. what is true of one type of work is not necessarily true of other types of work

3. Of the following traits, the one that is LEAST essential for the "ideal" supervisor is that she
   A. be consistent in her interpretation of the rules and policies of the agency for which she works
   B. is able to judge a person's ability at her first meeting with that person
   C. know her own job thoroughly
   D. appreciate and acknowledge honest effort and above-average work

4. The one of the following which is generally the basic reason for using standard procedure is to
   A. serve as a basis for formulating policies
   B. provide the sequence of steps for handling recurring activities
   C. train new employees in the policies and objectives
   D. facilitate periodic review of standard practices

5. An employee, while working at the bookkeeping machine, accidentally kicks off the holdup alarm system. She notifies the supervisor that she can hear the holdup alarm bell ringing, and requests that the holdup alarm system be reset. After the holdup alarm system has been reset, the supervisor should notify the manager that the alarm
   A. is in proper working order
   B. should be shut off while the employee is working the bookkeeping machine to avoid another such accident
   C. kick-plate should be moved away from the worker's reception window so that it cannot be set off accidentally
   D. should be relocated so that it cannot be heard in the bookkeeping office

6. A supervisor who spends a considerate amount of time correcting subordinates' procedural errors should consider FIRST the possibility of
   A. disciplining those who make errors consistently
   B. instituting refresher training sessions
   C. redesigning work forms
   D. requesting that the requirements for entry-level jobs be changed

7. A supervisor has a subordinate who has been late the past four mornings. Of the following, the MOST important action for the supervisor to take FIRST is to
   A. read the rules concerning lateness to the employee in an authoritative manner
   B. give the subordinate a chance to explain the reason for his lateness
   C. tell the employee he must come in on time the next day
   D. ask the friends of the employee whether they can tell him the reason for the employee's lateness

8. During a conversation, a subordinate tells his supervisor about a family problem For the supervisor to give EXPLICIT advice to the subordinate would be
   A. *desirable*, primarily because a happy employee is more likely to be productive
   B. *undesirable*, primarily because the supervisor should not allow a subordinate to discuss personal problems
   C. *desirable*, primarily because their personal relations will show a marked improvement
   D. *undesirable*, primarily because a supervisor should not take responsibility for handling a subordinate's personal problem

9. As a supervisor, you have received instructions for a drastic change in the procedure for processing cases.
   Of the following, the approach which is MOST likely to result in acceptance of the change by your subordinates is for you to
   A. inform all subordinates of the change by written memo so that they will have guidelines to follow
   B. ask your superior to inform the unit members about the change at a staff meeting

C. recruit the most experienced employee in the unit to give individual instruction to the other unit members
D. discuss the change and the reasons for it with the staff so that they understand their role in its implementation

10. Of the following, the principle which should GENERALLY guide a supervisor in the training of employees under his supervision is that
    A. training of employees should be delegated to more experienced employees in the same title
    B. primary emphasis should be placed on training for future assignments
    C. the training process should be a highly individual matter
    D. training efforts should concentrate on employees who have the greatest potential

10.____

KEY (CORRECT ANSWERS)

1.	B	6.	B
2.	B	7.	B
3.	B	8.	D
4.	B	9.	D
5.	D	10.	C

INTERPRETING STATISTICAL DATA GRAPHS, CHARTS AND TABLES

EXAMINATION SECTION

TEST 1

DIRECTIONS: Each question or incomplete statement is followed by several suggested answers or completions. Select the one that BEST answers the question or completes the statement. *PRINT THE LETTER OF THE CORRECT ANSWER IN THE SPACE AT THE RIGHT.*

Questions 1-8.

DIRECTIONS: Questions 1 through 8 are to be answered SOLELY on the basis of the information and chart given below.

The following chart shows expenses in five selected categories for a one-year period expressed as percentages of these same expenses during the previous year. The chart compares two different offices. In Office T (represented by [ ]) a cost reduction program has been tested for the past year. The other office, Office Q (represented by [////]) served as a control, in that no special effort was made to reduce costs during the past year.

RESULTS OF OFFICE COST REDUCTION PROGRAM

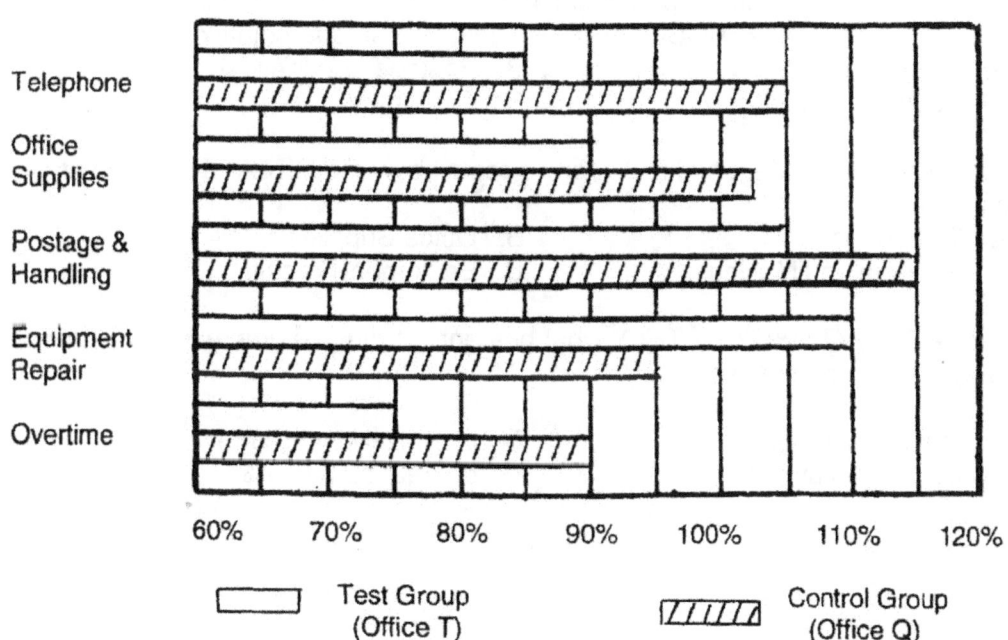

Expenses of Test and Control Groups for 2019
Expressed as Percentages of Same Expenses for 2018

2 (#1)

1. In Office T, which category of expenses showed the GREATEST percentage reduction from 2018 to 2019?
      A. Telephone
      B. Office Supplies
      C. Postage and Mailing
      D. Overtime

2. In which expense category did Office T show the BEST results in percentage terms when compared to Office Q?
      A. Telephone
      B. Office Supplies
      C. Postage and Mailing
      D. Overtime

3. According to the above chart, the cost reduction program was LEAST effective for the expense category of
      A. Office Supplies
      B. Postage and Mailing
      C. Equipment Repair
      D. Overtime

4. Office T's telephone costs went down during 2019 by APPROXIMATELY how many percentage points?
      A. 15
      B. 20
      C. 85
      D. 105

5. Which of the following changes occurred in expenses for Office Supplies in Office Q in the year 2019 as compared with the year 2018?
   They
      A. *increased* by more than 100%
      B. *remained* the same
      C. *decreased* by a few percentage points
      D. *increased* by a few percentage points

6. For which of the following expense categories do the results in Office T and the results in Office Q differ MOST NEARLY by 10 percentage points?
      A. Telephone
      B. Postage and Mailing
      C. Equipment Repair
      D. Overtime

7. In which expense category did Office Q's costs show the GREATEST percentage increase in 2019?
      A. Telephone
      B. Office Supplies
      C. Postage and Mailing
      D. Equipment Repair

8. In Office T, by APPROXIMATELY what percentage did overtime expense change during the past year?
   It
      A. *increased* by 15%
      B. *increased* by 75%
      C. *decreased* by 10%
      D. *decreased* by 25%

KEY (CORRECT ANSWERS)

1. D   5. D
2. A   6. B
3. C   7. C
4. A   8. D

TEST 2

DIRECTIONS: Each question or incomplete statement is followed by several suggested answers or completions. Select the one that BEST answers the question or completes the statement. *PRINT THE LETTER OF THE CORRECT ANSWER IN THE SPACE AT THE RIGHT.*

Questions 1-7.

DIRECTIONS: Questions 1 through 7 are to be answered SOLELY on the basis of the information contained in the following graph which relates to the work of a public agency.

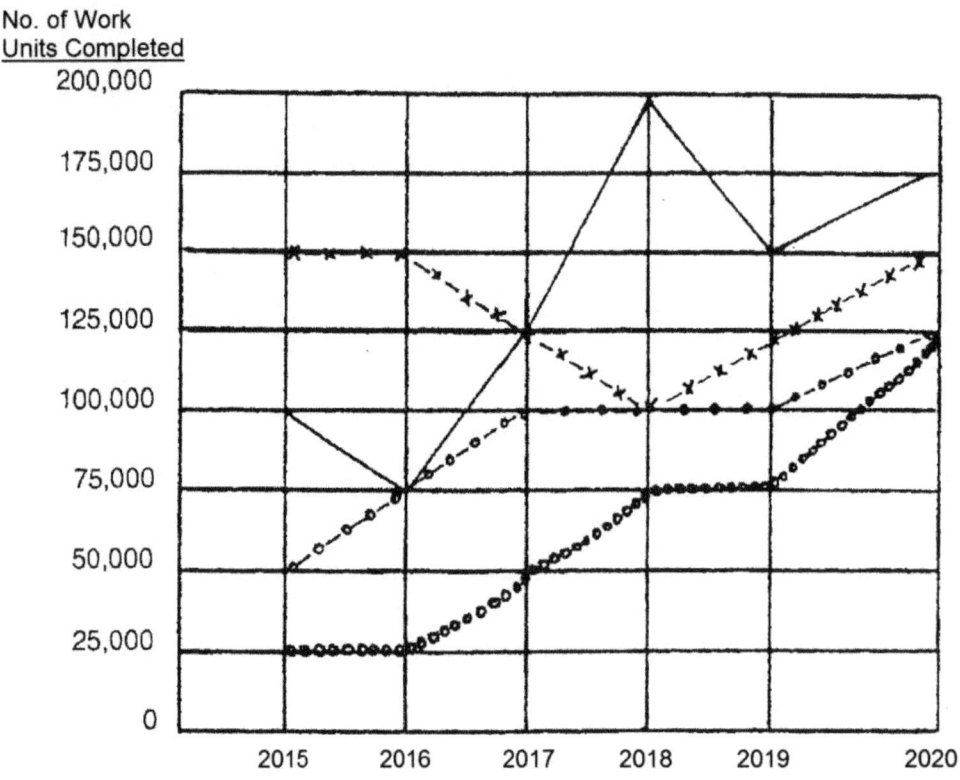

Units of each type of work completed by a public agency from 2015 to 2020.

Letters Written ─────
Documents Filed –x-x-x-x-x-x-x
Applications Processed -0-0-0-0-0
Inspections Made 0000000000000

1. The year for which the number of units of one type of work completed was less than it was for the previous year while the number of each of the other types of work completed was more than it was for the previous year was
   A. 2016   B. 2017   C. 2018   D. 2019

   1._____

2. The number of letters written exceeded the number of applications processed by the same amount in _____ of the years.
   A. two   B. three   C. four   D. five

   2._____

2 (#2)

3. The year in which the number of each type of work completed was GREATER than in the preceding year was
   A. 2017   B. 2018   C. 2019   D. 2020

   3._____

4. The number of applications processed and the number of documents filed were the SAME in
   A. 2016   B. 2017   C. 2018   D. 2019

   4._____

5. The TOTAL number of units of work completed by the agency
   A. increased in each year after 2015
   B. decreased from the prior year in two of the years after 2015
   C. was the same in two successive years from 2015 to 2020
   D. was less in 2015 than in any of the following years

   5._____

6. For the year in which the number of letters written was twice as high as it was in 2015, the number of documents filed was _____ it was in 2015.
   A. the same as   B. two-thirds of what
   C. five-sixths of what   D. one and one-half times what

   6._____

7. The variable which was the MOST stable during the period 2015 through 2020 was
   A. Inspections Made   B. Letters Written
   C. Documents Filed   D. Applications Processed

   7._____

KEY (CORRECT ANSWERS)

1. B   5. C
2. B   6. B
3. D   7. D
4. C

TEST 3

DIRECTIONS: Each question or incomplete statement is followed by several suggested answers or completions. Select the one that BEST answers the question or completes the statement. *PRINT THE LETTER OF THE CORRECT ANSWER IN THE SPACE AT THE RIGHT.*

Questions 1-10.

DIRECTIONS: Questions 1 through 10 are to be answered SOLELY on the basis of the REPORT OF TELEPHONE CALLS table given below.

	TABLE – REPORT OF TELEPHONE CALLS						
Dept.	No. of Stations	No. of Employees	No. of Incoming Calls In		No. of Long Distance Calls in		No. of Divisions
			2019	2020	2019	2020	
I	11	40	3421	4292	72	54	5
II	36	330	10392	10191	75	78	18
III	53	250	85243	85084	103	98	8
IV	24	60	9675	10123	82	85	6
V	13	30	5208	5492	54	48	6
VI	25	35	7472	8109	86	90	5
VII	37	195	11412	11299	68	72	11
VIII	36	54	8467	8674	59	68	4
IX	163	306	294321	289968	289	321	13
X	40	83	9588	8266	93	89	5
XI	24	68	7867	7433	86	87	13
XII	50	248	10039	10208	101	95	30
XIII	10	230	7550	6941	28	21	10
XVI	25	103	14281	14392	48	40	5
XV	19	230	8475	206	38	43	8
XVI	22	45	4684	5584	39	48	10
XVII	41	58	10102	9677	49	52	6
XVIII	82	106	106242	105889	128	132	10
XIX	6	13	2649	2498	35	29	2
XX	16	30	1395	1468	78	90	2

1. The department which had more than 106,000 incoming calls in 2019 but fewer than 250,000 is
   A. II B. IX C. XVIII D. III

   1.____

2. The department which has fewer than 8 divisions and more than 100 but fewer than 300 employees is
   A. VII B. XIV C. XV D. XVIII

   2.____

3. The department which had an increase in 2020 over 2019 in the number of both incoming and long distance calls but had an increase in long distance calls of not more than 3 was
   A. IV B. VI C. XVII D. XVIII

   3.____

2 (#3)

4. The department which had a decrease in the number of incoming calls in 2020 as compared to 2019 and has not less than 6 nor more than 7 divisions is
   A. IV B. V C. XVII D. III

   4.____

5. The department which has more than 7 divisions and more than 200 employees but fewer than 19 stations is
   A. XV B. III C. XX D. XIII

   5.____

6. The department having more than 10 divisions and fewer than 36 stations, which had an increase in long distance calls in 2020 over 2019, is
   A. XI B. VII C. XVI D. XVIII

   6.____

7. The department which in 2020 had at least 7,250 incoming calls and a decrease in long distance calls from 2019 and has more than 50 stations is
   A. IX B. XII C. XVIII D. III

   7.____

8. The department which has fewer than 25 stations, fewer than 100 employees, 10 or more divisions, and showed an increase of at least 9 long distance calls in 2020 over 2019 is
   A. IX B. XVI C. XX D. XIII

   8.____

9. The department which has more than 50 but fewer than 125 employees and had more than 5,000 incoming calls in 2019 but not more than 10,000, and more than 60 long distance calls in 2020 but not more than 85, and has more than 24 stations is
   A. VIII B. XIV C. IV D. XI

   9.____

10. If the number of departments showing an increase in long distance calls in 2020 over 1999 exceeds the number showing a decrease in long distance calls in the same period, select the Roman numeral indicating the department having less than one station for each 10 employees, provided not more than 8 divisions are served by that department.
    If the number of departments showing an increase in long distance calls in 2020 over 2019 does not exceed the number showing a decrease in long distance calls in the same period, select the Roman numeral indicating the department having the SMALLEST number of incoming calls in 2020.
    A. III B. XIII C. XV D. XX

    10.____

KEY (CORRECT ANSWERS)

1. C
2. B
3. A
4. C
5. D
6. A
7. D
8. B
9. A
10. C

TEST 4

DIRECTIONS: Each question or incomplete statement is followed by several suggested answers or completions. Select the one that BEST answers the question or completes the statement. *PRINT THE LETTER OF THE CORRECT ANSWER IN THE SPACE AT THE RIGHT.*

Questions 1-6.

DIRECTIONS: Questions 1 through 6 are to be answered SOLELY on the basis of the information given in the following chart. This chart shows the results of a study made of the tasks performed by a stenographer during one day. Included in the chart are the time at which she started a certain task and, under the particular heading, the amount of time, in minutes, she took to complete the task, and explanations of telephone calls and miscellaneous activities. NOTE: The time spent at lunch should not be included in any of your calculations.

PAMELA JOB STUDY							
NAME: Pamela Donald							DATE: 9/26
JOB TITLE: Stenographer						
DIVISION: Stenographic Pool						

Time of Start of Task	TASKS PERFORMED						Explanations of Telephone Calls and Miscellaneous Activities
	Taking Dictation	Typing	Filing	Telephone Work	Handling Mail	Misc. Activities	
9:00					22		
9:22						13	Picking up supplies
9:35						15	Cleaning typewriter
9:50	11						
10:01		30					
10:31				8			Call to Agency A
10:39	12						
10:51			10				
11:01				7			Call from Agency B
11:08		30					
11:38	10						
11:48				12			Call from Agency C
12:00	L U N C H						
1:00					28		
1:28	13						
1:41-2:13		32		12			Call to Agency B
X			15				
Y		50					
3:30	10						
3:40			21				
4:01				9			Call from Agency A
4:10	35						
4:45			9				
4:54						6	Cleaning up desk

95

2 (#4)

SAMPLE QUESTION:
The total amount of time spent on miscellaneous activities in the morning is exactly equal to the total amount of time spent
    A. filing in the morning
    B. handling mail in the afternoon
    C. miscellaneous activities in the afternoon
    D. handling mail in the morning

Explanation of answer to sample question:
The total amount of time spent on miscellaneous activities in the morning equals 28 minutes (13 minutes for picking up supplies plus 15 minutes for cleaning the typewriter); and since it takes 28 minutes to handle mail in the afternoon, the answer is B.

1. The time labeled Y at which the stenographer started a typing assignment was
    A. 2:15   B. 2:25   C. 2:40   D. 2:50

2. The ratio of time spent on all incoming calls to time spent on all outgoing calls for the day was
    A. 5:7   B. 5:12   C. 7:5   D. 7:12

3. Of the following combinations of tasks, which ones take up exactly 80% of the total time spent on Tasks Performed during the day?
    A. Typing, Filing, Telephone Work, Handling Mail
    B. Taking Dictation, Filing, and Miscellaneous Activities
    C. Taking Dictation, Typing, Handling Mail, and Miscellaneous Activities
    D. Taking Dictation, Typing, Filing, and Telephone Work

4. The total amount of time spent transcribing or typing work is how much MORE than the total amount of time spent in taking dictation?
    A. 55 minutes   B. 1 hour
    C. 1 hour 10 minutes   D. 1 hour 25 minutes

5. The GREATEST number of shifts in activities occurred between the times of
    A. 9:00 A.M. and 10:31 A.M.   B. 9:35 A.M. and 11:01 A.M.
    C. 10:31 A.M. and 12:00 Noon   D. 3:30 P.M. and 5:00 P.M.

6. The total amount of time spent on Taking Dictation in the morning plus the total amount of time spent on Filing in the afternoon is exactly EQUAL to the total amount of time spent on
    A. Typing in the afternoon minus the total amount of time spent on Telephone Work in the afternoon
    B. Typing in the morning plus the total amount of time spent on Miscellaneous Activities
    C. Dictation in the afternoon plus the total amount of time spent on Filing in the morning
    D. Typing in the afternoon minus the total amount of time spent in Handling Mail in the morning

KEY (CORRECT ANSWERS)

1. C
2. C
3. D
4. B
5. C
6. D

TEST 5

DIRECTIONS: Each question or incomplete statement is followed by several suggested answers or completions. Select the one that BEST answers the question or completes the statement. *PRINT THE LETTER OF THE CORRECT ANSWER IN THE SPACE AT THE RIGHT.*

Questions 1-8.

DIRECTIONS: Questions 1 through 8 are to be answered SOLELY on the basis of the information given in the following table.

	Bronx		Brooklyn		Manhattan		Queens		Richmond	
	May	June	May	June	May	June	May	June	May	June
Number of Clerks in Office Assigned To Issue Applications for Licenses	3	4	6	8	6	8	3	5	2	4
Number of Licenses Issued	950	1010	1620	1940	1705	2025	895	1250	685	975
Amount Collected in License Fees	$42,400	$52,100	$77,600	$94,500	$83,700	$98,800	$39,300	$65,500	$30,600	$48,200
Number of Inspectors	4	5	6	7	7	8	4	5	2	4
Number of Inspections Made	420	450	630	710	690	740	400	580	320	440
Number of Violations Found As a Result of Inspections	211	153	352	378	320	385	256	304	105	247

1. Of the following statements, the one which is NOT accurate on the basis of an inspection of the information contained in the table is that, for each office, the increase from May to June in the number of
   A. inspectors was accompanied by an increase in the number of inspections made
   B. licenses issued was accompanied by an increase in the amount collected in license fees
   C. inspections made was accompanied by an increase in the number of violations found
   D. licenses issued was accompanied by an increase in the number of clerks assigned to issue applications for licenses

   1.____

2. The TOTAL number of licenses issued by all five offices in the Division in May was
   A. 4,800   B. 5,855   C. 6,865   D. 7,200

   2.____

3. The total number of inspectors in all five borough offices in June exceeded the number in May by MOST NEARLY
   A. 21%   B. 26%   C. 55%   D. 70%

   3.____

4. In the month of June, the number of violations found per inspection made was the HIGHEST in
   A. Brooklyn   B. Manhattan   C. Queens   D. Richmond

5. In the month of May, the average number of inspections made by an inspector in the Bronx was the same as the average number of inspections made by an inspector in
   A. Brooklyn   B. Manhattan   C. Queens   D. Richmond

6. Assume that in June all of the inspectors in the Division spent 7 hours a day making inspections on each of the 21 working days in the month.
   Then the average amount of time that an inspector in the Manhattan office spent on an inspection that month was MOST NEARLY
   A. 2 hours
   B. 1 hour and 35 minutes
   C. 1 hour and 3 minutes
   D. 38 minutes

7. If an average fine of $100 was imposed for a violation found by the Division, what was the TOTAL amount in fines imposed for all the violations found by the Division in May?
   A. $124,400   B. $133,500   C. $146,700   D. $267,000

8. Assume that the amount collected in license fees by the entire Division in May was 80 percent of the amount collected by the entire Division in April.
   How much was collected by the entire Division in April?
   A. $218,880   B. $328,320   C. $342,000   D. $410,400

KEY (CORRECT ANSWERS)

1.	C	5.	A
2.	B	6.	B
3.	B	7.	A
4.	D	8.	C

TEST 6

DIRECTIONS: Each question or incomplete statement is followed by several suggested answers or completions. Select the one that BEST answers the question or completes the statement. *PRINT THE LETTER OF THE CORRECT ANSWER IN THE SPACE AT THE RIGHT.*

Questions 1-8.

DIRECTIONS: Questions 1 through 8 are to be answered SOLELY on the basis of the information contained in the chart and table shown below, which relate to Bureau X in a certain public agency. The chart shows the percentage of the bureau's annual expenditures spent on equipment, supplies, and salaries for each of the years 2016-2020. The table shows the bureau's annual expenditures for each of the years 2016-2020.

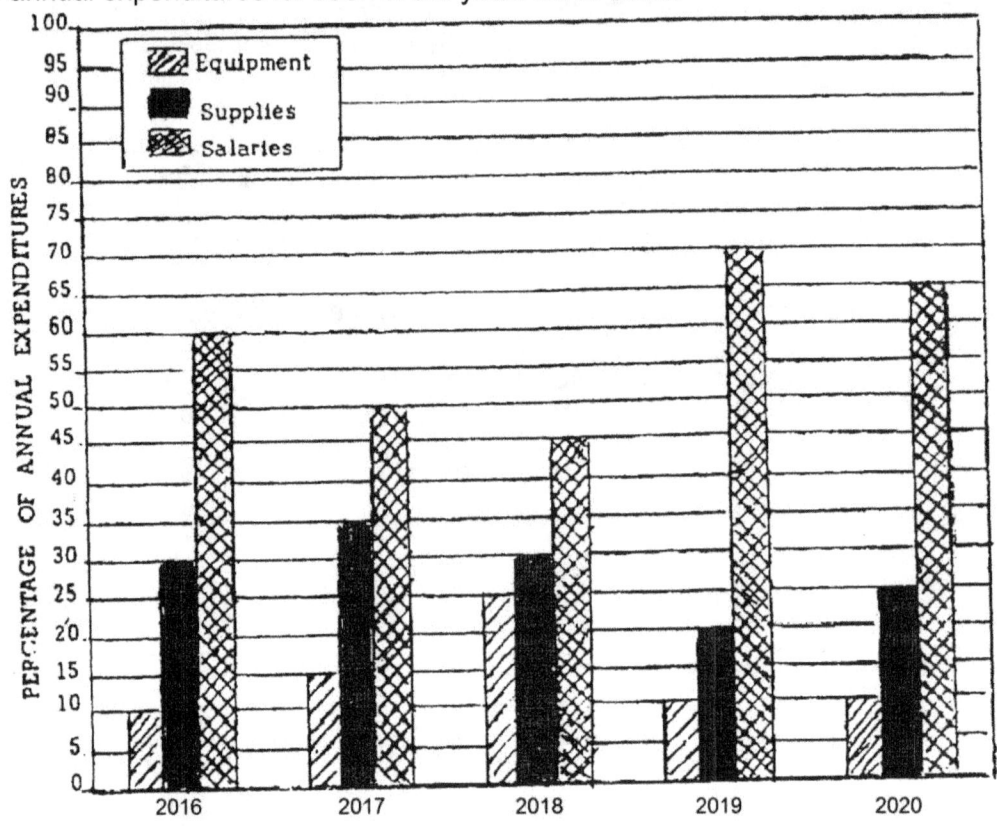

The bureau's annual expenditures for the years 2016-2020 are shown in the following table:

YEAR	EXPENDITURES
2016	$8,000,000
2017	$12,000,000
2018	$15,000,000
2019	$10,000,000
2020	$12,000,000

2 (#6)

Equipment, supplies, and salaries were the only three categories for which the bureau spent money.

Candidates may find it useful to arrange their computations on their scratch paper in an orderly manner since the correct computations for one question may also be helpful in answering another question.

1. The information contained in the chart and table is sufficient to determine the
   A. average annual salary of an employee in the bureau in 2017
   B. decrease in the amount of money spent on supplies in the bureau in 2016 from the amount spent in the preceding year
   C. changes between 2018 and 2019 in the prices of supplies bought by the bureau
   D. increase in the amount of money spent on salaries in the bureau in 2020 over the amount spent in the preceding year

   1.____

2. If the percentage of expenditures for salaries in one year is added to the percentage of expenditures for equipment in that year, a total of two percentages for that year is obtained.
   The two years for which this total is the SAME are
   A. 2016 and 2018   B. 2017 and 2019
   C. 2016 and 2019   D. 2017 and 2020

   2.____

3. Of the following, the year in which the bureau spent the GREATEST amount of money on supplies was
   A. 2020   B. 2018   C. 2016   D. 2016

   3.____

4. Of the following years, the one in which there was the GREATEST increase over the preceding year in the amount of money spent on salaries is
   A. 2019   B. 2020   C. 2016   D. 2018

   4.____

5. Of the bureau's expenditures for equipment in 2020, one-third was used for the purchase of mailroom equipment and the remainder was spent on miscellaneous office equipment.
   How much did the bureau spend on miscellaneous office equipment in 2020?
   A. $4,000,000   B. $400,000   C. $8,000,000   D. $800,000

   5.____

6. If there were 120 employees in the bureau in 2019, then the average annual salary paid to the employees in that year was MOST NEARLY
   A. $43,450   B. $49,600   C. $58,350   D. $80,800

   6.____

7. In 2018, the bureau had 125 employees.
   If 20 of the employees earned an average annual salary of $80,000, then the average salary of the other 105 employees was MOST NEARLY
   A. $49,000   B. $64,000   C. $41,000   D. $54,000

   7.____

3 (#6)

8. Assume that the bureau estimated that the amount of money it would spend on supplies in 2021 would be the same as the amount it spent on that category in 2020. Similarly, the bureau estimated that the amount of money it would spend on equipment in 2021 would be the same as the amount it spent on that category in 2020. However, the bureau estimated that in 2021 the amount it would spend on salaries would be 10 percent higher than the amount it spent on that category in 2020.
The percentage of its annual expenditures that the bureau estimated it would spend on supplies in 2021 is MOST NEARLY
   A. 27.5%   B. 23.5%   C. 22.5%   D. 25%

8._____

KEY (CORRECT ANSWERS)

1. D   5. D
2. A   6. C
3. B   7. A
4. C   8. B

PHILOSOPHY, PRINCIPLES, PRACTICES, AND TECHNICS OF SUPERVISION, ADMINISTRATION, MANAGEMENT, AND ORGANIZATION

TABLE OF CONTENTS

	Page
MEANING OF SUPERVISION	1
THE OLD AND THE NEW SUPERVISION	1
THE EIGHT (8) BASIC PRINCIPLES OF THE NEW SUPERVISION	1
I. Principle of Responsibility	1
II. Principle of Authority	2
III. Principle of Self-Growth	2
IV. Principle of Individual Worth	2
V. Principle of Creative Leadership	2
VI. Principle of Success and Failure	2
VII. Principle of Science	3
VIII. Principle of Cooperation	3
WHAT IS ADMINISTRATION?	3
I. Practices Commonly Classed as "Supervisory"	3
II. Practices Commonly Classed as "Administrative"	3
III. Practices Commonly Classed as Both "Supervisory" and "Administrative"	4
RESPONSIBILITIES OF THE SUPERVISOR	4
COMPETENCIES OF THE SUPERVISOR	4
THE PROFESSIONAL SUPERVISOR-EMPLOYEE RELATIONSHIP	4
MINI-TEXT IN SUPERVISION, ADMINISTRATION, MANAGEMENT, AND ORGANIZATION	5
I. Brief Highlights	5
A. Levels of Management	6
B. What the Supervisor Must Learn	6
C. A Definition of Supervision	6
D. Elements of the Team Concept	6
E. Principles of Organization	6
F. The Four Important Parts of Every Job	7
G. Principles of Delegation	7
H. Principles of Effective Communications	7
I. Principles of Work Improvement	7
J. Areas of Job Improvement	7
K. Seven Key Points in Making Improvements	8

L.	Corrective Techniques for Job Improvement	8
M.	A Planning Checklist	8
N.	Five Characteristics of Good Directions	9
O.	Types of Directions	9
P.	Controls	9
Q.	Orienting the New Employee	9
R.	Checklist for Orienting New Employees	9
S.	Principles of Learning	10
T.	Causes of Poor Performance	10
U.	Four Major Steps in On-the-Job Instructions	10
V.	Employees Want Five Things	10
W.	Some Don'ts in Regard to Praise	11
X.	How to Gain Your Workers' Confidence	11
Y.	Sources of Employee Problems	11
Z.	The Supervisor's Key to Discipline	11
AA.	Five Important Processes of Management	12
BB.	When the Supervisor Fails to Plan	12
CC.	Fourteen General Principles of Management	12
DD.	Change	12

II. Brief Topical Summaries 13
    A. Who/What is the Supervisor? 13
    B. The Sociology of Work 13
    C. Principles and Practices of Supervision 14
    D. Dynamic Leadership 14
    E. Processes for Solving Problems 15
    F. Training for Results 15
    G. Health, Safety, and Accident Prevention 16
    H. Equal Employment Opportunity 16
    I. Improving Communications 16
    J. Self-Development 17
    K. Teaching and Training 17
        1. The Teaching Process 17
            a. Preparation 17
            b. Presentation 18
            c. Summary 18
            d. Application 18
            e. Evaluation 18
        2. Teaching Methods 18
            a. Lecture 18
            b. Discussion 18
            c. Demonstration 19
            d. Performance 19
            e. Which Method to Use 19

PHILOSOPHY, PRINCIPLES, PRACTICES, AND TECHNICS OF SUPERVISION, ADMINISTRATION, MANAGEMENT, AND ORGANIZATION

MEANING OF SUPERVISION

The extension of the democratic philosophy has been accompanied by an extension in the scope of supervision. Modern leaders and supervisors no longer think of supervision in the narrow sense of being confined chiefly to visiting employees, supplying materials, or rating the staff. They regard supervision as being intimately related to all the concerned agencies of society, they speak of the supervisor's function in terms of "growth," rather than the "improvement" of employees.

This modern concept of supervision may be defined as follows: Supervision is leadership and the development of leadership within groups which are cooperatively engaged in inspection, research, training, guidance, and evaluation.

THE OLD AND THE NEW SUPERVISION

TRADITIONAL
1. Inspection
2. Focused on the employee
3. Visitation
4. Random and haphazard
5. Imposed and authoritarian
6. One person usually

MODERN
1. Study and analysis
2. Focused on aims, materials, methods, supervisors, employees, environment
3. Demonstrations, intervisitation, workshops, directed reading, bulletins, etc.
4. Definitely organized and planned (scientific)
5. Cooperative and democratic
6. Many persons involved (creative)

THE EIGHT (8) BASIC PRINCIPLES OF THE NEW SUPERVISION

I. Principle of Responsibility
   Authority to act and responsibility for acting must be joined.
   A. If you give responsibility, give authority.
   B. Define employee duties clearly.
   C. Protect employees from criticism by others.
   D. Recognize the rights as well as obligations of employees.
   E. Achieve the aims of a democratic society insofar as it is possible within the area of your work.
   F. Establish a situation favorable to training and learning.
   G. Accept ultimate responsibility for everything done in your section, unit, office, division, department.
   H. Good administration and good supervision are inseparable.

II. Principle of Authority
The success of the supervisor is measured by the extent to which the power of authority is not used.
   A. Exercise simplicity and informality in supervision
   B. Use the simplest machinery of supervision
   C. If it is good for the organization as a whole, it is probably justified.
   D. Seldom be arbitrary or authoritative.
   E. Do not base your work on the power of position or of personality.
   F. Permit and encourage the free expression of opinions.

III. Principle of Self-Growth
The success of the supervisor is measured by the extent to which, and the speed with which, he is no longer needed.
   A. Base criticism on principles, not on specifics.
   B. Point out higher activities to employees.
   C. Train for self-thinking by employees to meet new situations.
   D. Stimulate initiative, self-reliance, and individual responsibility
   E. Concentrate on stimulating the growth of employees rather than on removing defects.

IV. Principle of Individual Worth
Respect for the individual is a paramount consideration in supervision.
   A. Be human and sympathetic in dealing with employees.
   B. Don't nag about things to be done.
   C. Recognize the individual differences among employees and seek opportunities to permit best expression of each personality.

V. Principle of Creative Leadership
The best supervision is that which is not apparent to the employee.
   A. Stimulate, don't drive employees to creative action.
   B. Emphasize doing good things.
   C. Encourage employees to do what they do best.
   D. Do not be too greatly concerned with details of subject or method.
   E. Do not be concerned exclusively with immediate problems and activities.
   F. Reveal higher activities and make them both desired and maximally possible.
   G. Determine procedures in the light of each situation but see that these are derived from a sound basic philosophy.
   H. Aid, inspire, and lead so as to liberate the creative spirit latent in all good employees.

VI. Principle of Success and Failure
There are no unsuccessful employees, only unsuccessful supervisors who have failed to give proper leadership.
   A. Adapt suggestions to the capacities, attitudes, and prejudices of employees.
   B. Be gradual, be progressive, be persistent.
   C. Help the employee find the general principle; have the employee apply his own problem to the general principle.
   D. Give adequate appreciation for good work and honest effort.
   E. Anticipate employee difficulties and help to prevent them.
   F. Encourage employees to do the desirable things they will do anyway.
   G. Judge your supervision by the results it secures.

VII. Principle of Science
Successful supervision is scientific, objective, and experimental. It is based on facts, not on prejudices.
- A. Be cumulative in results.
- B. Never divorce your suggestions from the goals of training.
- C. Don't be impatient of results.
- D. Keep all matters on a professional, not a personal, level.
- E. Do not be concerned exclusively with immediate problems and activities.
- F. Use objective means of determining achievement and rating where possible.

VIII. Principle of Cooperation
Supervision is a cooperative enterprise between supervisor and employee.
- A. Begin with conditions as they are.
- B. Ask opinions of all involved when formulating policies.
- C. Organization is as good as its weakest link.
- D. Let employees help to determine policies and department programs.
- E. Be approachable and accessible—physically and mentally.
- F. Develop pleasant social relationships.

WHAT IS ADMINISTRATION

Administration is concerned with providing the environment, the material facilities, and the operational procedures that will promote the maximum growth and development of supervisors and employees. (Organization is an aspect and a concomitant of administration.)

There is no sharp line of demarcation between supervision and administration; these functions are intimately interrelated and, often, overlapping. They are complementary activities.

I. Practices Commonly Classed as "Supervisory"
- A. Conducting employees' conferences
- B. Visiting sections, units, offices, divisions, departments
- C. Arranging for demonstrations
- D. Examining plans
- E. Suggesting professional reading
- F. Interpreting bulletins
- G. Recommending in-service training courses
- H. Encouraging experimentation
- I. Appraising employee morale
- J. Providing for intervisitation

II. Practices Commonly Classified as "Administrative"
- A. Management of the office
- B. Arrangement of schedules for extra duties
- C. Assignment of rooms or areas
- D. Distribution of supplies
- E. Keeping records and reports
- F. Care of audio-visual materials
- G. Keeping inventory records
- H. Checking record cards and books

I. Programming special activities
J. Checking on the attendance and punctuality of employees

III. Practices Commonly Classified as Both "Supervisory" and "Administrative"
   A. Program construction
   B. Testing or evaluating outcomes
   C. Personnel accounting
   D. Ordering instructional materials

RESPONSIBILITIES OF THE SUPERVISOR

A person employed in a supervisory capacity must constantly be able to improve his own efficiency and ability. He represent the employer to the employees and only continuous self-examination can make him a capable supervisor.

Leadership and training are the supervisor's responsibility. An efficient working unit is one in which the employees work with the supervisor. It is his job to bring out the best in his employees. He must always be relaxed, courteous, and calm in his association with his employees. Their feelings are important, and a harsh attitude does not develop the most efficient employees.

COMPETENCES OF THE SUPERVISOR

I. Complete knowledge of the duties and responsibilities of his position.
II. To be able to organize a job, plan ahead, and carry through.
III. To have self-confidence and initiative.
IV. To be able to handle the unexpected situation and make quick decisions.
V. To be able to properly train subordinates in the positions they are best suited for.
VI. To be able to keep good human relations among his subordinates.
VII. To be able to keep good human relations between his subordinates and himself and to earn their respect and trust.

THE PROFESSIONAL SUPERVISOR-EMPLOYEE RELATIONSHIP

There are two kinds of efficiency: one kind is only apparent and is produced in organizations through the exercise of mere discipline; this is but a simulation of the second, or true, efficiency which springs from spontaneous cooperation. If you are a manager, no matter how great or small your responsibility, it is your job, in the final analysis, to create and develop this involuntary cooperation among the people whom you supervise. For, no matter how powerful a combination of money, machines, and materials a company may have, this is a dead and sterile thing without a team of willing, thinking, and articulate people to guide it.

The following 21 points are presented as indicative of the exemplary basic relationship that should exist between supervisor and employee:

1. Each person wants to be liked and respected by his fellow employee and wants to be treated with consideration and respect by his superior.
2. The most competent employee will make an error. However, in a unit where good relations exist between the supervisor and his employees, tenseness and fear do not exist. Thus, errors are not hidden or covered up, and the efficiency of a unit is not impaired.

3. Subordinates resent rules, regulations, or orders that are unreasonable or unexplained.
4. Subordinates are quick to resent unfairness, harshness, injustices, and favoritism.
5. An employee will accept responsibility if he knows that he will be complimented for a job well done, and not too harshly chastised for failure; that his supervisor will check the cause of the failure, and, if it was the supervisor's fault, he will assume the blame therefore. If it was the employee's fault, his supervisor will explain the correct method or means of handling the responsibility.
6. An employee wants to receive credit for a suggestion he has made, that is used. If a suggestion cannot be used, the employee is entitled to an explanation. The supervisor should not say "no" and close the subject.
7. Fear and worry slow up a worker's ability. Poor working environment can impair his physical and mental health. A good supervisor avoids forceful methods, threats, and arguments to get a job done.
8. A forceful supervisor is able to train his employees individually and as a team, and is able to motivate them in the proper channels.
9. A mature supervisor is able to properly evaluate his subordinates and to keep them happy and satisfied.
10. A sensitive supervisor will never patronize his subordinates.
11. A worthy supervisor will respect his employees' confidences.
12. Definite and clear-cut responsibilities should be assigned to each executive.
13. Responsibility should always be coupled with corresponding authority.
14. No change should be made in the scope or responsibilities of a position without a definite understanding to that effect on the part of all persons concerned.
15. No executive or employee, occupying a single position in the organization, should be subject to definite orders from more than one source.
16. Orders should never be given to subordinates over the head of a responsible executive. Rather than do this, the officer in question should be supplanted.
17. Criticisms of subordinates should, whoever possible, be made privately, and in no case should a subordinate be criticized in the presence of executives or employees of equal or lower rank.
18. No dispute or difference between executives or employees as to authority or responsibilities should be considered too trivial for prompt and careful adjudication.
19. Promotions, wage changes, and disciplinary action should always be approved by the executive immediately superior to the one directly responsible.
20. No executive or employee should ever be required, or expected, to be at the same time an assistant to, and critic of, another.
21. Any executive whose work is subject to regular inspection should, wherever practicable, be given the assistance and facilities necessary to enable him to maintain an independent check of the quality of his work.

MINI-TEXT IN SUPERVISION, ADMINISTRATION, MANAGEMENT, AND ORGANIZATION

I. Brief Highlights

Listed concisely and sequentially are major headings and important data in the field for quick recall and review.

A. Levels of Management
Any organization of some size has several levels of management. In terms of a ladder, the levels are:

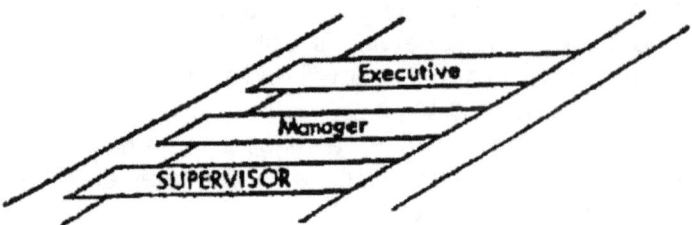

The first level is very important because it is the beginning point of management leadership.

B. What the Supervisor Must Learn
A supervisor must learn to:
1. Deal with people and their differences
2. Get the job done through people
3. Recognize the problems when they exist
4. Overcome obstacles to good performance
5. Evaluate the performance of people
6. Check his own performance in terms of accomplishment

C. A Definition of Supervisor
The term supervisor means any individual having authority, in the interests of the employer, to hire, transfer, suspend, lay-off, recall, promote, discharge, assign, reward, or discipline other employees or responsibility to direct them, or to adjust their grievances, or effectively to recommend such action, if, in connection with the foregoing, exercise of such authority is not of a merely routine or clerical nature but requires the use of independent judgment.

D. Elements of the Team Concept
What is involved in teamwork? The component parts are:
1. Members
2. A leader
3. Goals
4. Plans
5. Cooperation
6. Spirit

E. Principles of Organization
1. A team member must know what his job is.
2. Be sure that the nature and scope of a job are understood.
3. Authority and responsibility should be carefully spelled out.
4. A supervisor should be permitted to make the maximum number of decisions affecting his employees.
5. Employees should report to only one supervisor.
6. A supervisor should direct only as many employees as he can handle effectively.
7. An organization plan should be flexible.

8. Inspection and performance of work should be separate.
9. Organizational problems should receive immediate attention.
10. Assign work in line with ability and experience.

F. The Four Important Parts of Every Job
1. Inherent in every job is the *accountability* for results.
2. A second set of factors in every job is *responsibilities*.
3. Along with duties and responsibilities one must have the *authority* to act within certain limits without obtaining permission to proceed.
4. No job exists in a vacuum. The supervisor is surrounded by key *relationships*.

G. Principles of Delegation
Where work is delegated for the first time, the supervisor should think in terms of these questions:
1. Who is best qualified to do this?
2. Can an employee improve his abilities by doing this?
3. How long should an employee spend on this?
4. Are there any special problems for which he will need guidance?
5. How broad a delegation can I make?

H. Principles of Effective Communications
1. Determine the media.
2. To whom directed?
3. Identification and source authority.
4. Is communication understood?

I. Principles of Work Improvement
1. Most people usually do only the work which is assigned to them.
2. Workers are likely to fit assigned work into the time available to perform it.
3. A good workload usually stimulates output.
4. People usually do their best work when they know that results will be reviewed or inspected.
5. Employees usually feel that someone else is responsible for conditions of work, workplace layout, job methods, type of tools/equipment, and other such factors.
6. Employees are usually defensive about their job security.
7. Employees have natural resistance to change.
8. Employees can support or destroy a supervisor.
9. A supervisor usually earns the respect of his people through his personal example of diligence and efficiency.

J. Areas of Job Improvement
The areas of job improvement are quite numerous, but the most common ones which a supervisor can identify and utilize are:
1. Departmental layout
2. Flow of work
3. Workplace layout
4. Utilization of manpower
5. Work methods
6. Materials handling

7. Utilization
8. Motion economy

K. Seven Key Points in Making Improvements
   1. Select the job to be improved
   2. Study how it is being done now
   3. Question the present method
   4. Determine actions to be taken
   5. Chart proposed method
   6. Get approval and apply
   7. Solicit worker participation

L. Corrective Techniques of Job Improvement
   Specific Problems
   1. Size of workload
   2. Inability to meet schedules
   3. Strain and fatigue
   4. Improper use of men and skills
   5. Waste, poor quality, unsafe conditions
   6. Bottleneck conditions that hinder output
   7. Poor utilization of equipment and machine
   8. Efficiency and productivity of labor

   General Improvement
   1. Departmental layout
   2. Flow of work
   3. Work plan layout
   4. Utilization of manpower
   5. Work methods
   6. Materials handling
   7. Utilization of equipment
   8. Motion economy

   Corrective Techniques
   1. Study with scale model
   2. Flow chart study
   3. Motion analysis
   4. Comparison of units produced to standard allowance
   5. Methods analysis
   6. Flow chart and equipment study
   7. Down time vs. running time
   8. Motion analysis

M. A Planning Checklist
   1. Objectives
   2. Controls
   3. Delegations
   4. Communications
   5. Resources
   6. Manpower

7. Equipment
8. Supplies and materials
9. Utilization of time
10. Safety
11. Money
12. Work
13. Timing of improvements

N. Five Characteristics of Good Directions
In order to get results, directions must be:
1. Possible of accomplishment
2. Agreeable with worker interests
3. Related to mission
4. Planned and complete
5. Unmistakably clear

O. Types of Directions
1. Demands or direct orders
2. Requests
3. Suggestion or implication
4. volunteering

P. Controls
A typical listing of the overall areas in which the supervisor should establish controls might be:
1. Manpower
2. Materials
3. Quality of work
4. Quantity of work
5. Time
6. Space
7. Money
8. Methods

Q. Orienting the New Employee
1. Prepare for him
2. Welcome the new employee
3. Orientation for the job
4. Follow-up

R. Checklist for Orienting New Employees   Yes   No
1. Do you appreciate the feelings of new employees when they first report for work?   ___   ___
2. Are you aware of the fact that the new employee must make a big adjustment to his job?   ___   ___
3. Have you given him good reasons for liking the job and the organization?   ___   ___
4. Have you prepared for his first day on the job?   ___   ___
5. Did you welcome him cordially and make him feel needed?   ___   ___

	Yes	No

    6. Did you establish rapport with him so that he feels free to talk and discuss matters with you?
    7. Did you explain his job to him and his relationship to you?
    8. Does he know that his work will be evaluated periodically on a basis that is fair and objective?
    9. Did you introduce him to his fellow workers in such a way that they are likely to accept him?
   10. Does he know what employee benefits he will receive?
   11. Does he understand the importance of being on the job and what to do if he must leave his duty station?
   12. Has he been impressed with the importance of accident prevention and safe practice?
   13. Does he generally know his way around the department?
   14. Is he under the guidance of a sponsor who will teach the right way of doing things?
   15. Do you plan to follow-up so that he will continue to adjust successfully to his job?

S. Principles of Learning
   1. Motivation
   2. Demonstration or explanation
   3. Practice

T. Causes of Poor Performance
   1. Improper training for job
   2. Wrong tools
   3. Inadequate directions
   4. Lack of supervisory follow-up
   5. Poor communications
   6. Lack of standards of performance
   7. Wrong work habits
   8. Low morale
   9. Other

U. Four Major Steps in On-The-Job Instruction
   1. Prepare the worker
   2. Present the operation
   3. Tryout performance
   4. Follow-up

V. Employees Want Five Things
   1. Security
   2. Opportunity
   3. Recognition
   4. Inclusion
   5. Expression

W. Some Don'ts in Regard to Praise
1. Don't praise a person for something he hasn't done.
2. Don't praise a person unless you can be sincere.
3. Don't be sparing in praise just because your superior withholds it from you.
4. Don't let too much time elapse between good performance and recognition of it

X. How to Gain Your Workers' Confidence
Methods of developing confidence include such things as:
1. Knowing the interests, habits, hobbies of employees
2. Admitting your own inadequacies
3. Sharing and telling of confidence in others
4. Supporting people when they are in trouble
5. Delegating matters that can be well handled
6. Being frank and straightforward about problems and working conditions
7. Encouraging others to bring their problems to you
8. Taking action on problems which impede worker progress

Y. Sources of Employee Problems
On-the-job causes might be such things as:
1. A feeling that favoritism is exercised in assignments
2. Assignment of overtime
3. An undue amount of supervision
4. Changing methods or systems
5. Stealing of ideas or trade secrets
6. Lack of interest in job
7. Threat of reduction in force
8. Ignorance or lack of communications
9. Poor equipment
10. Lack of knowing how supervisor feels toward employee
11. Shift assignments

Off-the-job problems might have to do with:
1. Health
2. Finances
3. Housing
4. Family

Z. The Supervisor's Key to Discipline
There are several key points about discipline which the supervisor should keep in mind:
1. Job discipline is one of the disciplines of life and is directed by the supervisor.
2. It is more important to correct an employee fault than to fix blame for it.
3. Employee performance is affected by problems both on the job and off.
4. Sudden or abrupt changes in behavior can be indications of important employee problems.
5. Problems should be dealt with as soon as possible after they are identified.
6. The attitude of the supervisor may have more to do with solving problems than the techniques of problem solving.
7. Correction of employee behavior should be resorted to only after the supervisor is sure that training or counseling will not be helpful.

8. Be sure to document your disciplinary actions.
9. Make sure that you are disciplining on the basis of facts rather than personal feelings.
10. Take each disciplinary step in order, being careful not to make snap judgments, or decisions based on impatience.

AA. Five Important Processes of Management
1. Planning
2. Organizing
3. Scheduling
4. Controlling
5. Motivating

BB. When the Supervisor Fails to Plan
1. Supervisor creates impression of not knowing his job
2. May lead to excessive overtime
3. Job runs itself—supervisor lacks control
4. Deadlines and appointments missed
5. Parts of the work go undone
6. Work interrupted by emergencies
7. Sets a bad example
8. Uneven workload creates peaks and valleys
9. Too much time on minor details at expense of more important tasks

CC. Fourteen General Principles of Management
1. Division of work
2. Authority and responsibility
3. Discipline
4. Unity of command
5. Unity of direction
6. Subordination of individual interest to general interest
7. Remuneration of personnel
8. Centralization
9. Scalar chain
10. Order
11. Equity
12. Stability of tenure of personnel
13. Initiative
14. Esprit de corps

DD. Change

Bringing about change is perhaps attempted more often, and yet less well understood, than anything else the supervisor does. How do people generally react to change? (People tend to resist change that is imposed upon them by other individuals or circumstances.

Change is characteristic of every situation. It is a part of every real endeavor where the efforts of people are concerned.

1. Why do people resist change?
   People may resist change because of:
   a. Fear of the unknown
   b. Implied criticism
   c. Unpleasant experiences in the past
   d. Fear of loss of status
   e. Threat to the ego
   f. Fear of loss of economic stability

2. How can we best overcome the resistance to change?
   In initiating change, take these steps:
   a. Get ready to sell
   b. Identify sources of help
   c. Anticipate objections
   d. Sell benefits
   e. Listen in depth
   f. Follow up

II. Brief Topical Summaries

   A. Who/What is the Supervisor?
      1. The supervisor is often called the "highest level employee and the lowest level manager."
      2. A supervisor is a member of both management and the work group. He acts as a bridge between the two.
      3. Most problems in supervision are in the area of human relations, or people problems.
      4. Employees expect: Respect, opportunity to learn and to advance, and a sense of belonging, and so forth.
      5. Supervisors are responsible for directing people and organizing work. Planning is of paramount importance.
      6. A position description is a set of duties and responsibilities inherent to a given position.
      7. It is important to keep the position description up-to-date and to provide each employee with his own copy.

   B. The Sociology of Work
      1. People are alike in many ways; however, each individual is unique.
      2. The supervisor is challenged in getting to know employee differences. Acquiring skills in evaluating individuals is an asset.
      3. Maintaining meaningful working relationships in the organization is of great importance.
      4. The supervisor has an obligation to help individuals to develop to their fullest potential.
      5. Job rotation on a planned basis helps to build versatility and to maintain interest and enthusiasm in work groups.
      6. Cross training (job rotation) provides backup skills.

7. The supervisor can help reduce tension by maintaining a sense of humor, providing guidance to employees, and by making reasonable and timely decisions. Employees respond favorably to working under reasonably predictable circumstances.
8. Change is characteristic of all managerial behavior. The supervisor must adjust to changes in procedures, new methods, technological changes, and to a number of new and sometimes challenging situations.
9. To overcome the natural tendency for people to resist change, the supervisor should become more skillful in initiating change.

C. Principles and Practices of Supervision
1. Employees should be required to answer to only one superior.
2. A supervisor can effectively direct only a limited number of employees, depending upon the complexity, variety, and proximity of the jobs involved.
3. The organizational chart presents the organization in graphic form. It reflects lines of authority and responsibility as well as interrelationships of units within the organization.
4. Distribution of work can be improved through an analysis using the "Work Distribution Chart."
5. The "Work Distribution Chart" reflects the division of work within a unit in understandable form.
6. When related tasks are given to an employee, he has a better chance of increasing his skills through training.
7. The individual who is given the responsibility for tasks must also be given the appropriate authority to insure adequate results.
8. The supervisor should delegate repetitive, routine work. Preparation of recurring reports, maintaining leave and attendance records are some examples.
9. Good discipline is essential to good task performance. Discipline is reflected in the actions of employees on the job in the absence of supervision.
10. Disciplinary action may have to be taken when the positive aspects of discipline have failed. Reprimand, warning, and suspension are examples of disciplinary action.
11. If a situation calls for a reprimand, be sure it is deserved and remember it is to be done in private.

D. Dynamic Leadership
1. A style is a personal method or manner of exerting influence.
2. Authoritarian leaders often see themselves as the source of power and authority.
3. The democratic leader often perceives the group as the source of authority and power.
4. Supervisors tend to do better when using the pattern of leadership that is most natural for them.
5. Social scientists suggest that the effective supervisor use the leadership style that best fits the problem or circumstances involved.
6. All four styles—telling, selling, consulting, joining—have their place. Using one does not preclude using the other at another time.

7. The theory X point of view assumes that the average person dislikes work, will avoid it whenever possible, and must be coerced to achieve organizational objectives.
8. The theory Y point of view assumes that the average person considers work to be a natural as play, and, when the individual is committed, he requires little supervision or direction to accomplish desired objectives.
9. The leader's basic assumptions concerning human behavior and human nature affect his actions, decisions, and other managerial practices.
10. Dissatisfaction among employees is often present, but difficult to isolate. The supervisor should seek to weaken dissatisfaction by keeping promises, being sincere and considerate, keeping employees informed, and so forth.
11. Constructive suggestions should be encouraged during the natural progress of the work.

E. Processes for Solving Problems
1. People find their daily tasks more meaningful and satisfying when they can improve them.
2. The causes of problems, or the key factors, are often hidden in the background. Ability to solve problems often involves the ability to isolate them from their backgrounds. There is some substance to the cliché that some persons "can't see the forest for the trees."
3. New procedures are often developed from old ones. Problems should be broken down into manageable parts. New ideas can be adapted from old one.
4. People think differently in problem-solving situations. Using a logical, patterned approach is often useful. One approach found to be useful includes these steps:
    a. Define the problem
    b. Establish objectives
    c. Get the facts
    d. Weigh and decide
    e. Take action
    f. Evaluate action

F. Training for Results
1. Participants respond best when they feel training is important to them.
2. The supervisor has responsibility for the training and development of those who report to him.
3. When training is delegated to others, great care must be exercised to insure the trainer has knowledge, aptitude, and interest for his work as a trainer.
4. Training (learning) of some type goes on continually. The most successful supervisor makes certain the learning contributes in a productive manner to operational goals.
5. New employees are particularly susceptible to training. Older employees facing new job situations require specific training, as well as having need for development and growth opportunities.
6. Training needs require continuous monitoring.
7. The training officer of an agency is a professional with a responsibility to assist supervisors in solving training problems.

8. Many of the self-development steps important to the supervisor's own growth are equally important to the development of peers and subordinates. Knowledge of these is important when the supervisor consults with others on development and growth opportunities.

G. Health, Safety, and Accident Prevention
1. Management-minded supervisors take appropriate measures to assist employees in maintaining health and in assuring safe practices in the work environment.
2. Effective safety training and practices help to avoid injury and accidents.
3. Safety should be a management goal. All infractions of safety which are observed should be corrected without exception.
4. Employees' safety attitude, training and instruction, provision of safe tools and equipment, supervision, and leadership are considered highly important factors which contribute to safety and which can be influenced directly by supervisors.
5. When accidents do occur, they should be investigated promptly for very important reasons, including the fact that information which is gained can be used to prevent accidents in the future.

H. Equal Employment Opportunity
1. The supervisor should endeavor to treat all employees fairly, without regard to religion, race, sex, or national origin.
2. Groups tend to reflect the attitude of the leader. Prejudice can be detected even in very subtle form. Supervisors must strive to create a feeling of mutual respect and confidence in every employee.
3. Complete utilization of all human resources is a national goal. Equitable consideration should be accorded women in the work force, minority-group members, the physically and mentally handicapped, and the older employee. The important question is: "Who can do the job?"
4. Training opportunities, recognition for performance, overtime assignments, promotional opportunities, and all other personnel actions are to be handled on an equitable basis.

I. Improving Communications
1. Communications is achieving understanding between the sender and the receiver of a message. It also means sharing information—the creation of understanding.
2. Communication is basic to all human activity. Words are means of conveying meanings; however, real meanings are in people.
3. There are very practical differences in the effectiveness of one-way, impersonal, and two-way communications. Words spoken face-to-face are better understood. Telephone conversations are effective, but lack the rapport of person-to-person exchanges. The whole person communicates.
4. Cooperation and communication in an organization go hand in hand. When there is a mutual respect between people, spelling out rules and procedures for communicating is unnecessary.
5. There are several barriers to effective communications. These include failure to listen with respect and understanding, lack of skill in feedback, and misinterpreting the meanings of words used by the speaker. It is also common

practice to listen to what we want to hear, and tune out things we do not want to hear.
6. Communication is management's chief problem. The supervisor should accept the challenge to communicate more effectively and to improve interagency and intra-agency communications.
7. The supervisor may often plan for and conduct meetings. The planning phase is critical and may determine the success or the failure of a meeting.
8. Speaking before groups usually requires extra effort. Stage fright may never disappear completely, but it can be controlled.

J. Self-Development
1. Every employee is responsible for his own self-development.
2. Toastmaster and toastmistress clubs offer opportunities to improve skills in oral communications.
3. Planning for one's own self-development is of vital importance. Supervisors know their own strengths and limitations better than anyone else.
4. Many opportunities are open to aid the supervisor in his developmental efforts, including job assignments; training opportunities, both governmental and non-governmental—to include universities and professional conferences and seminars.
5. Programmed instruction offers a means of studying at one's own rate.
6. Where difficulties may arise from a supervisor's being away from his work for training, he may participate in televised home study or correspondence courses to meet his self-development needs.

K. Teaching and Training
1. The Teaching Process
Teaching is encouraging and guiding the learning activities of students toward established goals. In most cases this process consists of five steps: preparation, presentation, summarization, evaluation, and application.

   a. Preparation
   Preparation is two-fold in nature; that of the supervisor and the employee. Preparation by the supervisor is absolutely essential to success. He must know what, when, where, how, and whom he will teach. Some of the factors that should be considered are:
   1) The objectives
   2) The materials needed
   3) The methods to be used
   4) Employee participation
   5) Employee interest
   6) Training aids
   7) Evaluation
   8) Summarization

   Employee preparation consists in preparing the employee to receive the material. Probably the most important single factor in the preparation of the employee is arousing and maintaining his interest. He must know the objectives of the training, why he is there, how the material can be used, and its importance to him.

b. Presentation
   In presentation, have a carefully designed plan and follow it. The plan should be accurate and complete, yet flexible enough to meet situations as they arise. The method of presentation will be determined by the particular situation and objectives.

c. Summary
   A summary should be made at the end of every training unit and program. In addition, there may be internal summaries depending on the nature of the material being taught. The important thing is that the trainee must always be able to understand how each part of the new material relates to the whole.

d. Application
   The supervisor must arrange work so the employee will be given a chance to apply new knowledge or skills while the material is still clear in his mind and interest is high. The trainee does not really know whether he has learned the material until he has been given a chance to apply it. If the material is not applied, it loses most of its value.

e. Evaluation
   The purpose of all training is to promote learning. To determine whether the training has been a success or failure, the supervisor must evaluate this learning.
   In the broadest sense, evaluation includes all the devices, methods, skills, and techniques used by the supervisor to keep himself and the employees informed as to their progress toward the objectives they are pursuing. The extent to which the employee has mastered the knowledge, skills, and abilities, or changed his attitudes, as determined by the program objectives, is the extent to which instruction has succeeded or failed.
   Evaluation should not be confined to the end of the lesson, day, or program but should be used continuously. We shall note later the way this relates to the rest of the teaching process.

2. Teaching Methods
   A teaching method is a pattern of identifiable student and instructor activity used in presenting training material.
   All supervisors are faced with the problem of deciding which method should be used at a given time.

   a. Lecture
      The lecture is direct oral presentation of material by the supervisor. The present trend is to place less emphasis on the trainer's activity and more on that of the trainee.

   b. Discussion
      Teaching by discussion or conference involves using questions and other techniques to arouse interest and focus attention upon certain areas, and by doing so creating a learning situation. This can be one of the most

valuable methods because it gives the employees an opportunity to express their ideas and pool their knowledge.

   c. Demonstration
The demonstration is used to teach how something works or how to do something. It can be used to show a principle or what the results of a series of actions will be. A well-staged demonstration is particularly effective because it shows proper methods of performance in a realistic manner.

   d. Performance
Performance is one of the most fundamental of all learning techniques or teaching methods. The trainee may be able to tell how a specific operation should be performed but he cannot be sure he knows how to perform the operation until he has done so.
As with all methods, there are certain advantages and disadvantages to each method.

   e. Which Method to Use
Moreover, there are other methods and techniques of teaching. It is difficult to use any method without other methods entering into it. In any learning situation, a combination of methods is usually more effective than any one method alone.

Finally, evaluation must be integrated into the other aspects of the teaching-learning process.

It must be used in the motivation of the trainees; it must be used to assist in developing understanding during the training; and it must be related to employee application of the results of training.

This is distinctly the role of the supervisor.

www.ingramcontent.com/pod-product-compliance
Lightning Source LLC
Chambersburg PA
CBHW082209300426
44117CB00016B/2730